SERVE STRONG

BUT

STAY SANE

TEN MISTAKES THAT WILL RUIN YOUR MISSION—OR LIFE

Gary G Taylor, Ph.D.

River Oaks
Publishing

ISBN 978-0-692-72114-8

Printed in the United States of America

First Edition June 2016

10 9 8 7 6 5 4 3 2 1

About the Author: Dr. Taylor is a life-long member of the Church of Jesus Christ of Latter-day Saints.   He has served in many positions in the Church, his favorite being a teacher.   Dr. Taylor earned a PhD in psychology from Brigham Young University and has been in private practice for over forty years. He is now retired and he and his wife Melody live in St. George, Utah.   They have ten children and twenty-four grandchildren. Dr. Taylor served a two year proselyting mission years ago in the Canadian Mission; and he and his wife Melody have served together on two eighteen month missions in the Europe and South Pacific Area offices.   During this time, Dr. Taylor was an Area Mental Advisor working with hundreds of missionaries who were struggling during their service.

CONTENTS

INTRODUCTION

A friend told me about an experience he had as a young missionary a number of years ago while serving in Germany. He had been in Germany about two months when he had an extremely vivid dream in which he saw himself back home with his family and friends. It was a glorious experience in which he was warm, happy, loved, safe, and very much at peace in his dream. Then he woke to the reality of the shabby apartment he shared with his hard-to-get-along-with missionary companion. It was freezing cold; and it was his turn to get up and get the coal fired furnace and water heater going. He was looking at another day with not much on the agenda other than knocking on doors in the frigid cold; and facing the often equally frigid treatment from those behind the doors he knocked on. Worst of all, there were twenty-two long months to go before he could return home. As he lay there in great misery, my friend had the almost serious thought: "I only have two choices. I think I'll flip a coin. Heads I'll kill myself; and tails I'll get up and go tracting."

My friend laughs about it now; but he wasn't laughing at the time. This was an exceptionally painful moment that tested his faith and resolve like never before in his life. After some soul searching, he chose to get up and get on with his mission; which along with additional painful moments, included many experiences that were enriching, fun, and fulfilling. His was an experience typical of most missionaries. Along with being discouraged, fatigued, bored, and disillusioned at times, most missionaries are alternately inspired, strengthened, and they have moments of pure

5

joy. They typically come home with marvelous stories of changed lives and spiritual enlightenment; but enduring a daily grind is often the cost of these priceless experiences. As one of my grandsons wrote about his mission in South Africa, "It has been the most humbling, frustrating, annoying, best, happiest, worst, greatest thing you could ever imagine. But I cherish every single second of it".

Along with being physically exhausting, most missionaries find that serving a full-time mission is a great challenge from an emotional/mental health standpoint. Not only is the work unusually demanding; but normal coping strategies previously employed to deal with emotional pressures are not available. A missionary under stress is not free to go off and be alone while he works out the problem. He can't go for a long run when he chooses, read a novel, play a video game or easily call on family and special friends at home for support. Of course, support from family and friends is generally available and can be very helpful; but it's clearly not the same when limited to letters, weekly email, or twice a year phone calls. While serving a full-time mission, any preexisting inclination to anxiety, depression, or any other mental health problem is likely to be triggered. Ongoing problems brought into the mission field are exacerbated. And, like my friend, at least mild mental health problems, usually anxiety and depression, are very likely to arise occasionally even in those who have never before been troubled.

This said, the majority of missionaries resolve the inevitable emotional and mental health challenges inherent in missionary work and are able to complete successful missions. The struggle is healthy and leaves them with stronger faith and a better understanding of how to use the powers of heaven in their lives. They end up better equipped to be successful in family, career and other pursuits in their life going forward. Another piece of good news is that those who find the experience overwhelming can get the help they need. Most importantly as a source of help, missionaries have access to spiritual strength and direction like never before in their lives. But other resources are also available.

Among these is a self-help booklet entitled "Adjusting to Missionary Life" published by the Church in 2013. This is a wonderful resource developed over several years by LDS mental health experts; and then carefully reviewed by General Authorities. This booklet is published in several languages and is available in all missions throughout the world. There are many current and former missionaries who claim to have found this booklet to be a great help. Those interested can access the booklet by the Internet using the Missionary Portal (lds.org/callings/missionary); or a copy can be purchased using the Internet website (store.lds.org).

Serving missionaries who experience debilitating mental health problems can also receive professional treatment while serving. In many areas of the world, this service is provided through LDS Family Services, or other local mental health professionals. There are also mental health professionals on call through the Missionary Department; as well as Area Mental Health Advisors serving in most areas of the world. Area Mental Health Advisors are Senior Missionaries who have professional experience and credentials. They are called through the same process, and work under the same conditions as do all Senior Missionaries; but their specific calling is to advise Mission Presidents regarding mental health issues, to insure that adequate local help is provided to missionaries where available, and/or to provide pastoral counseling themselves—all of which when requested by a Mission President. Although "talking with a shrink" is not high on a typical missionary's agenda, it is nice to know that the service is generally available when needed. It also helps when the "shrink" in question has more in common with a priesthood leader than a professional counselor.

My wife and I had the privilege of serving as Mental Health Advisors in both the Europe and Pacific Areas. In the three years of this service, we saw firsthand how difficult missionary service can be; but also how much the Lord loves and helps those who dedicate themselves in His service. I'm not sure how else to explain the success in our work. Almost all contact with missionaries was by telephone, which had its obvious limitations. Along with the absence of in-person visual contact, connections were often less than desirable; and language and cultural barriers made the experience even more difficult. Yet, communication was generally possible and the result positive. Any number of times we had the experience of learning more than we were teaching. It was a common experience when talking to missionaries to have impressions and ideas come to mind that were novel and unanticipated. I remember often thinking as new ideas would come to mind, "Wow! That's interesting. I would never have thought that."

In our experience, Mission Presidents and their wives, as well as General Authorities on mission visits, were also inspired, often in dramatic ways. Even though they typically didn't have mental health training, my wife and I saw many instances in which they were inspired to say just the right thing, or make just the right adjustment in a missionary's assignment, in order to help a struggling missionary. We also noticed times in which it seemed like a particular missionary was assigned to exactly the right Mission President—one who by personality and approach was uniquely qualified to help an individual missionary.

Of course, in spite of the help available to struggling missionaries, there are times when the nature of a mental health problem is such that it cannot be adequately resolved while a missionary continues to serve. In the areas I served, about ten percent of all missionaries were referred for professional counselling in any given year; and of those referred for counselling, the great majority had problems that could be resolved in a few counseling sessions. That left a relatively small percentage of missionaries (although significant in actual numbers) with problems of the type that required a return home for treatment.

In my experience, the missionaries who needed to return home had a difficult time accepting the fact. These young men and women were generally committed to their missions and had given it their all. They, of course, wanted resolution of their health problems; but they also wanted to continue their service. These conflicting desires, as well as family concerns, often made this a traumatic experience for the missionaries and their families. A description of how the decision is made to send a missionary home early; and ideas on how to minimize the potential trauma are given later in Chapter Eleven.

But what about the great majority, even including those with diagnosed mental health conditions, who are able to complete successful missions? What do they do that allows them to adjust to, and even thrive under, the stress of missionary work? In my experience working with about 1200 missionaries, several factors became obvious that can make all the difference. Specifically, it became apparent that missionaries do much better if they do the following ten things well:

1. Have realistic expectations.
2. Avoid worry about things that are beyond their control.
3. Avoid absolute thinking and making absolute, argumentative comments to companions and others.
4. Focus on what's right, not what's wrong about themselves, their work, and everything in between.
5. Trust God and have a vision of the "Big Picture".
6. Strive for perfection but avoid perfectionism.
7. Manage themselves and others according to priesthood principles.
8. Learn to manage fear and anger well.
9. Become really good at forgiving.
10. Invest fully in their mission and don't too often take the easy way out.

The intent of this book is to discuss these and other factors using scripture and actual case examples. The hope is to offer practical suggestions regarding how missionaries can better implement the principles involved in successful missions, both in their missionary service and throughout life.

The intended audience for this book includes potential and serving missionaries, and those who care about them; but you will likely notice that the concepts advanced are as relevant to general life struggles as they are to missionary work. All readers can benefit from a review of the principles discussed. These principles are universal and easy to understand; but not always easy to apply. Constant reminders and continued effort are necessary to keep these principles present and working throughout our lives. The discussion begins with the first common mistake made by many missionaries. That is, having unrealistic expectations.

Please note that all the case examples which follow are factual; but names have been changed and certain circumstances altered to protect the privacy of those involved.

It should also be understood that the interpretations of scripture and the overall content of this book represent the opinion of the author. They do not represent the official position of the Church of Jesus Christ of Latter-day Saints.

CHAPTER ONE

MISTAKE ONE: HAVING UNREALISTIC EXPECTATIONS

It had been an unusual day for President Wright. All of the basically non-stop calls he received relative to his responsibilities as Mission President had been positive. There had been no major problems requiring his attention. Until that is, a late night call from one of the young Sister missionaries in the mission. It took a while to get it out, and there were a lot of tears in the process, but she was finally able to say, "I'm so sorry President. I just can't do this anymore. Please, let me go home". This was by no means the first time he had received a call like this; but it was a shock to receive the call from Sister Green. She was an excellent missionary who had been serving for almost a year with no apparent problems. So why was she experiencing this unexpected crisis?

As the story evolved, it became clear that Sister Green had become disillusioned and depressed in large part because of a common mistake made by a number of missionaries. She came into the field with several unreasonable expectations for both herself and her mission. When comparing her performance on her mission to these unreasonable expectations, she had become convinced that her mission was a failure. It was apparent to her that her best effort was not good enough. In her view, she obviously didn't have what it takes to be a successful missionary.

And by extension, she assumed she would also fail as a wife and mother; and in all other aspects of her life.

It took some time; but with consultation from her Mission President, a Mental Health Advisor, and confirmation from the Spirit, this young missionary was able to adjust her expectations in a way that allowed her to see the truth about her mission and herself. She was able to continue serving and she began to experience more of what she had hoped to gain from her mission. Specifically, her unrealistic expectations and the ways in which she changed her thinking were as follows:

Unrealistic Expectation: With enough faith and exact obedience, any missionary will find converts, no matter the circumstances or where they are called to serve.

Fridays were often the worst day of the week for Sister Green. Friday was the day her District Leader requested their Call-in Summary Report. She was also quite uncomfortable in most District and Zone meetings; and when attending ward council meetings or interacting with her local ward leaders. The problem was that, in spite of working very hard, she and her companion taught relatively few lessons each week and they currently had no progressing investigators with firm baptismal dates. This reality contrasted with the expectation she felt from her mission leaders; and also from what she herself expected would happen on her mission.

The situation differs from mission to mission, and even from area to area within a given mission; but many missionaries feel pressure to have baptisms. Sometimes this pressure comes from mission leaders who promise baptisms if missionaries are sufficiently faithful and obedient. In other cases, the pressure comes more from within the missionary. Whatever the source, when dealing with this kind of pressure, it's helpful if missionaries have the following perspective:

Obedience and faith are necessary in order to have a successful mission; but they do not guarantee a large number of baptisms. The truth is that missionaries who are obedient to mission rules and who exercise great faith will be more successful; and they will get more out of their mission. In general, they will also typically find and baptize more converts than others who are less committed. As discussed in more detail later, for a number of reasons, it is critically important that missionaries be prepared to serve with all of their heart, might, mind and strength (D&C 4). On the other hand, fulfilling this requirement does not guarantee that a missionary will baptize no matter what the circumstance.

As an example, we read in the Book of Mormon about the mission of Ammon and the great success he had (see Alma 17 thru 20). At the same time, his brother Aaron was serving in a different area. Not only did Aaron and his associates not have converts during this period, they were imprisoned and suffered greatly. No doubt Aaron had as much faith and was as committed to his mission as was Ammon; but Aaron and his colleagues served under a very different set of circumstances. As we read in the Book of Mormon, "...it was their lot to have fallen into the hands of a more hardened and a more stiff-necked people; therefore they would not hearken unto their words..." (Alma 20:30).

Following the example of Aaron, a number of modern-day missionaries have also had great faith, been exactly obedient, and put forth great effort, without experiencing many baptisms during their service. One famous example of this is President Hinckley. In her biography of President Hinckley, Sheri Dew gives details of the thousands of pamphlets distributed and the dedication Elder Hinckley demonstrated during his mission (Sheri Dew, G*o Forward with Faith: the Biography of Gordon B. Hinckley*, Deseret Book, 1996). There is no doubt that he also exercised great faith. Even so, he experienced few if any baptisms. The truth is that you can be a very successful missionary and yet not have any or many baptisms. This is as true of missionaries today as it was when Joseph Smith offered the following promise to missionaries who didn't have a lot of success in his day, "if you do your duty, it will be just as well with you as if all men embraced the gospel" (Joseph Smith, Letter to the Church, 1833, Joseph Smith Papers, ID 1458).

The primary goal of a mission is to invite as many people as possible to come to Christ. Whether or not those invited accept the invitation is beyond a missionary's control. Stated exactly, a missionary's purpose is to "Invite others to come unto Christ by helping them receive the restored gospel through faith in Jesus Christ and His Atonement, repentance, baptism, receiving the gift of the Holy Ghost, and enduring to the end" (Preach My Gospel, p. 1). One of the key words in this mission statement is "invite", not insure or force. Making invitations is something that is largely within a missionary's control. Once invited, responsibility to accept the invitation obviously moves to those invited. As we read in Matthew "...how often would I have gathered my children together, even as a hen gathereth her chickens under her wings, and ye would not!" (Matthew 23:37). Even the perfect missionary, the Savior Himself, found many who would not accept His message.

The goal then is to serve with full purpose of heart and mind, which naturally leads to exact obedience and maximum effort, in inviting and helping as many people as possible come to Christ. Once accomplished, a mission is successful with or without a large tally of baptisms. Conversely, if missionaries fail to serve diligently, their missions are not successful, no matter how many baptisms they have. For one thing, when they fail to serve diligently, missionaries themselves are not likely to become converts; which is a primary hope in missionary service. As I have heard it expressed by several General Authorities in different settings, the dramatic increase in missionaries sparked when the age of missionary service was lowered in 2013, was not motivated by a need to increase convert baptisms; but rather by a desire to save the rising generation. Missions served faithfully can do that. The hallmark of successful missions is reached when returned missionaries remain obedient and become a spiritual force throughout their life; and when their children and grandchildren become committed disciples.

Unrealistic Expectation: A missionary will (should) feel the Spirit at all times.

Virtually all missionaries understand, as instructed in numerous scriptures and Preach My Gospel (PMG), that "the message of the Restoration of the gospel must be taught by divine power…" (PMG, p.3). They understand how indispensable having the Spirit is in all aspects of their missionary service. They are familiar with the emphatic statement made by the Lord found in the Doctrine and Covenants: "And the Spirit shall be given unto you by the prayer of faith; and if ye receive not the Spirit ye shall not teach." (D & C 42:14). Missionaries generally also hear testimonies from other missionaries about how they so frequently feel the Spirit in their work and have dramatic experiences as a result. Sister Green knew about and had heard all of this; but she was not having the experience she expected. She did feel the Spirit at times, and she recognized minor miracles and sometimes major ones; but not to the degree or nearly as often as she expected. In her experience she was most often just "going through the motions", robot-like, with no obvious inspiration or warm feelings.

To her credit, this fact didn't cause Sister Green to doubt the Spirit, or the importance of the work she was doing. But it did lead her to conclude that there was something wrong with her. "I must not be praying with enough faith." "There is obviously something wrong with me or my approach." It wasn't until she rethought the situation that everything began to make sense. The following ideas were a part of that rethinking process.

Missionaries can have the Spirit in their work, but they may not feel it. If a person is praying earnestly for the Spirit; and if that person is basically worthy; it's reasonable to assume that he or she will absolutely have the Spirit in their righteous endeavors. To believe otherwise would seem to contradict our understanding of who God is and how He works with us. As the Savior pointed out in the Sermon on the Mount: "Or what man is there of you, who if his son ask bread, will give him a stone? Or if he ask a fish, will he give him a serpent? If ye then, being evil, know how to give good gifts unto your children, how much more shall your Father who is in heaven give good things to them that ask him." (3 Nephi

17

14:9-11). Given this truth, it's inconceivable that missionaries like Sister Green who are dedicated to the service of God, and who pray earnestly for divine direction, would not be granted the Spirit in their work.

On the other hand, it's quite possible that a missionary might not be aware of having the Spirit, even when it's present. This apparently happened to a group of Lamanites who had faith in the Savior, had been converted, baptized, and had received the Holy Ghost, but *"they knew it not"* (3 Nephi, 9:20, italics added). This is always a possibility because learning to recognize spiritual promptings, and developing the ability to distinguish them from similar experiences, is no simple matter. It takes effort and time to learn. As Elder Richard G. Scott has taught, there is a good reason for this. "Our Father expects us to learn how to obtain that divine help by exercising faith in Him and in His Holy Son. Were we to receive inspired guidance just for the asking, we would become weak and ever more dependent on Him. He knows that essential personal growth will come as we struggle to learn how to be led by the spirit" (Richard G. Scott, "To Acquire Spiritual Guidance", *Ensign*, November, 2009).

Along with it being a difficult skill to develop generally, it's also true that being depressed, anxious, or distracted can limit our ability to recognize communication from the Spirit. As President Boyd K Packer taught, "The Spirit does not get our attention by shouting or shaking us with a heavy hand. Rather it whispers. It caresses so gently that if we are preoccupied we may not feel it at all" ("The Candle of the Lord." *Ensign*, January. 1983, 53). In Sister Green's case, continual negative thinking about herself and worry about her performance was blocking those sensitive spiritual feelings. Ironically, she was so concerned about not feeling the Spirit; that in itself was a big part of the reason she wasn't. In short, Sister Green did have the Spirit with her; but for several reasons, she didn't recognize its influence.

In terms of how the Spirit works with us, we are told in the Doctrine and Covenants, "Yea, behold, I will tell you in your mind and in your heart, by the Holy Ghost, which shall come upon you and which shall dwell in your heart" (D&C 8:2). The term "mind" used in this and other scripture, seems to refer to intellectual processes in our brain, such as perception, learning, memory, and attitudes, by which we process information. The term "heart", when used in scripture, seems to refer to feelings or emotion. Centers of emotion are, of course, also located in the brain, not the heart. But the centers in the brain responsible for feelings, and the processes involved by which emotions are created and managed, are quite different from those involved in general intellectual function. Emotions also have a different impact on how we behave. It therefore makes sense that general intellectual processes and emotion would be distinguished from each other in scriptural references. The metaphors of heart and mind make this distinction nicely. However defined, the relevant suggestion here is that the Spirit communicates with us using our natural faculties.

That being the case, it's easy to see how distraction, disease, or any number of natural factors could interfere with this process. Satan likely also uses these same natural processes when he tempts us. Sister Green was beyond Satan's influence when it came to tempting her to break mission rules, or do anything that would be morally inappropriate; but she was susceptible to believing that the Spirit wasn't available to her, and that her best efforts were not good enough. This lie from the "father of lies" (Moses 4:4) provided a seed bed for negative conclusions about her worth and the work she was doing. It also took a lot of her focus and effort to process. Finally, it had triggered depression and anxiety; which will inevitably dampen one's spiritual experience in their own right. Mental health problems alone, of course, don't affect worthiness, or the presence of the Spirit in our lives; but they often do limit our ability to feel that presence.

Perhaps the difficulty inherent when mortals seek to receive and understand divine guidance is the basic reason for the fact that "in the mouth of two or three witnesses shall every word be established" (D&C 6:28). We can't assume that feeling strongly about something means that it must be true; nor can we trust something to be true simply because of how much sense it makes intellectually. Essentially we have these two largely independent internal witnesses to consider when seeking divine direction; and they both need to agree. These two internal witnesses then need to be checked against the external witness of truth found in scripture and through priesthood leaders who hold the appropriate keys. When all three agree, there is good reason to assume that we have the truth. Sister Green experienced strong feelings of failure, but that impression was not confirmed by her Mission President, who held priesthood keys to make such judgements; nor, did it make sense intellectually; at least when she took the time to think carefully about it. The emotion was strong, but obviously misguided.

Even when engaged in the service of the Lord, inspiration will not always be provided. This is true for several reasons. For example, there may be times when missionaries don't receive inspiration because what they would naturally do, based on their own understanding and experience, is entirely appropriate. This was apparently the case with two early missionaries. "Wherefore, go ye and preach my gospel, whether to the north or to the south, to the east or to the west, it mattereth not, for ye cannot go amiss (D&C 80:3). Sister Green and her companions were always doing their best to preach the gospel; and that desire and intent meant that the decisions they made on their own initiative were usually acceptable to the Lord. Sister Green also had a year of experience as a missionary at this point. During that year she had learned a lot and grown considerably in her teaching ability and people skills. Therefore, inspiration was not as often needed as it had been earlier in her service. For these reasons she didn't feel the Spirit as often as she did when she first began her mission; or as often as she thought she should. Perhaps this wasn't so much a problem as it was evidence of the Lord's confidence in her.

There may also be times when missionaries are not inspired because there is nothing that they can do that will affect the outcome. For example, if two missionaries have prayerfully prepared for a lesson, and are teaching with a prayer in their heart, it's safe to assume that they will be inspired to say just the right thing (D&C 100:6); or remember the perfect scripture, *assuming that doing so would make a difference to those they are teaching.* But those being taught may not be open to the Spirit or ready for what is being taught. Or the "perfect" scripture in the mind of the missionary might in fact not be the perfect scripture for the investigator. In those cases, there is again, no real need for the inspiration sought.

21

Furthermore, there may also be other times when we are left on our own because acting on our own in a particular situation will help us learn an important lesson; and/or it may be part of the testing experience that life is intended to be (Abraham 3:25). I remember as a young missionary having the assignment to drive a visiting General Authority to a mission conference. My companion and I hadn't communicated properly and I thought the conference was to be held in a chapel on the West side of Toronto, Canada; when in fact, it was scheduled for a meeting house on the East side. Before the error became obvious, we had traveled a good ways in the wrong direction in rush hour traffic. As a result, the General Authority, was an hour late for the meeting. One might expect that given the importance of the General Authority's time; not to mention the time of all the missionaries assembled for the conference, inspiration would have been provided to avoid the mistake. My companion and I had certainly prayed for help with our responsibilities relative to the conference; but no such luck. The good news is that this unfortunate incident taught my companion and me an important lesson on planning and communication; not to mention the test of patience it provided for the Mission President and the visiting General Authority.

For all of these reasons, worthy missionaries will not always receive the revelation they seek; which is apparently just as it should be. As Elder Dallin H. Oaks has taught, "The Lord's way puts limits on how often He will speak to us by His Spirit. Not understanding this, some have been misled by expecting too much revelation...We believe in continuing revelation, not continuous revelation" (Dallin H. Oaks, "In His Own Time, in His Own Way", *Ensign*, August, 2013). Likewise from Elder Boyd K. Packer, "I have learned that strong, impressive spiritual experiences do not come to us very frequently" (Boyd K Packer, *That All May be Edified*, Deseret Book, 1982, p.337). The Lord knows what we need in all circumstances, and He will provide what is needed in all cases; but not necessarily what is expected.

Unrealistic Expectation: The Church has a perfect history. There have been no mistakes in doctrine or procedure. Any doubts about any aspect of the Church or its doctrine are inappropriate and dangerous.

As Sister Green grew up, religious discussions were primarily with family, seminary teachers, and others who shared a gospel testimony. Once in the field, she started hearing for the first time in a negative way about multiple accounts of the First Vision, details about Joseph Smith's marriages, the Mountain Meadows Massacre and other issues that critics love to raise. This new information proved to be troubling and difficult to process. Her basic testimony remained intact. She had experienced too many answers to prayer and had too much faith in what she did know about the Church for that to become a problem.

At the same time, the new information did lead her to question herself. She was alarmed thinking that she couldn't be a good missionary if she had any doubts or questions in her mind; and her new doubts led her to worry that she was on the road to apostasy. In other words, she knew that she had not lost her testimony, but she was concerned that she might. All of this worry was disconcerting and took attention away from the positive aspects of her work. Sister Green reworked her understanding in the following ways:

Many missionaries, Church leaders, and other faithful members have questions about some aspect of Church policy or doctrine. As President Uchtdorf rather famously said in his October, 2013 conference address, "please, first doubt your doubts before you doubt your faith. We must never allow doubt to hold us prisoner and keep us from the divine love, peace, and gifts that come through faith in the Lord Jesus Christ" ("Come Join With Us", *Ensign*, November, 2013). This is great advice; and it applies at one time or another to most of us.

President Uchtdorf in the same conference address, also said, "There are few members of the Church who, at one time or another have not wrestled with serious or sensitive questions. One of the purposes of the Church is to nurture and cultivate the seed of faith—even in the sometimes sandy soil of doubt and uncertainty. Faith is the hope for things which are not seen but which are true." As President Uchtdorf explains, it's healthy and natural to have doubts at times when we are talking about matters of faith, for which there is by definition no definitive proof.

Over time, many of our questions are answered as new information and experience come along. In the meantime, however, it makes sense to focus on what we do know and believe. Good missionaries teach and bear witness of the basic essentials of the gospel; which virtually all of them believe in strongly. It's not necessary to teach or profess things that are not understood or believed.

Doubts arise for good reasons, including the fact that mistakes have been made by Church leaders in the past. In the October 2013 conference address referred to above, President

Uchtdorf also mentioned three primary reasons for the doubts that members might have. The first problem he mentions was alluded to earlier. We simply do not have all of the information needed to understand everything perfectly. When the whole truth is known, things will make sense to us that don't now. But in the meantime, questions and even doubts are natural. A second problem is that there can be a difference of opinion about what "facts" mean, even when the facts are known. It's interesting how the same "facts" lead to such different conclusions when discussed by the Church's critics as opposed to its apologists. It can be disconcerting when a missionary hears only the critics take on the facts.

Lastly, President Uchtdorf indicates that mistakes have been made in the past. Along with teaching so much that is right, even prophets and apostles have gotten a few things wrong in their beliefs and teaching. Quoting President Uchtdorf, "God is perfect, and His doctrine is pure. But He works through us—His imperfect children—and imperfect people make mistakes…this is the way it has always been and will be until the perfect day when Christ Himself reigns personally upon the earth." Putting this in terms of a common metaphor, there is bound to be a little bath water in the tub along with the baby. Recognizing and discarding the bath water makes sense; but there is no reason to throw the baby out as well. Nor is there any good reason to claim that there is no bath water at all; or as in Sister Green's case, to feel guilty when there are things that make no sense to us, or seem wrong. Those concerns need to be prayerfully and patiently worked out; but meanwhile, there is no need for doubts and questions to interfere with our missionary or other service in the Church. As stated above, a missionary simply needs to stay focused on the basics, in which virtually all missionaries have a solid testimony.

25

Unrealistic Expectation: With sufficient preparation and inspiration, a missionary can answer all investigator questions.

Sister Green would also often feel inadequate and unprepared when she wasn't able to answer an investigator's questions to their satisfaction. And if a lesson didn't go well, she was quick to blame herself. She was operating on the false assumption that if she and her companion did things right, she would know how to answer all questions raised by investigators, and all lessons would be wonderfully productive. The truth was, and generally is, a bit different.

There is no way to answer questions in a way that will be satisfying to all investigators. In His wisdom, there are many things in the gospel that have not yet been revealed. For example, we don't know why the priesthood is restricted to men, or why polygamy has been a part of God's plan at times. Many have speculated about answers to these and similar questions; but answers have not been clearly revealed. When questions about such things come up, there is certainly no need for a missionary to feel inadequate or guilty about not having an answer, or to be concerned in any way about the gap in knowledge. A simple comment such as, "I don't have an answer for that; but here is what I do know", followed by continuing to teach basic doctrine, will suffice. In fact, that is far better than sharing speculation and getting off track in a lesson.

It also helps to remember that things are revealed "line upon line, precept upon precept" (Isaiah 28:10), all in God's wisdom. After all, He has done this before (Moses 1:33) and He certainly knows what He is doing. It's important for us all to forgo requiring God to explain Himself to our satisfaction. We need to allow Him to rule the universe and be content with the many things we may not yet understand and cannot control.

Even when missionaries are adequately prepared and bring the Spirit to their teaching, investigators may not be in a position to benefit. Naturally, some investigators simply are not prepared or willing to understand the things of God. In Isaiah we read, "For my thoughts are not your thoughts, neither are your ways my ways, saith the Lord. For as the heavens are higher than the earth, so are my ways higher than your ways, and my thoughts than your thoughts" (Isaiah 55:8-9). Those who are insufficiently humble, and/or aren't willing to do their part in developing faith, will not be satisfied with a missionary's responses no matter how effective the missionary. Therefore, there is no reason to believe that just because a lesson doesn't go well a missionary must have done an inadequate job. Even the Savior, the perfect teacher, was not always able to get those He taught to understand and accept His teachings.

Unrealistic expectation: If I am willing to serve a mission, I will be blessed to overcome my problems and all of my prayers will be answered.

There were instances in which Sister Green knew that her prayers had been heard and answered. But at the same time, there were instances in which she felt her prayers were not answered. This often happens in the case of missionaries who have problems that have not been resolved prior to their mission. As an example, one Elder was extremely shy before his mission. It was virtually impossible for him to speak in public, or be the center of attention in any way. He assumed that if he agreed to serve a mission, the Lord would remove his social anxiety. He was disappointed and confused by the fact that his problem wasn't much better after several months on his mission. Another Elder had a pornography problem which he expected would magically disappear if he chose to serve a mission. It didn't. A Sister missionary suffered from depression for most of her young life. She had assumed that she would find relief while serving; when in fact, her depression deepened. All of these missionaries had assumed a blessing that God had not actually promised. The truth is:

God will not do for us what we must do for ourselves. In some cases, mental health problems involve brain chemistry, or some combination of physiological issues, that make controlling our thoughts impossible. In most cases, however, even those struggling with significant mental health issues have a degree of control over what they dwell on in their thinking. Where that is true, God cannot solve the problem without overruling our agency; which He cannot, or at least will not, do (2 Nephi 2:27). Relative to the three missionaries mentioned above, anyone will become depressed, even full-time servants of the Lord, if they consistently choose to think negative, pessimistic thoughts. If pornographic thoughts are entertained, encouraged, and relished, addictions will persist. If a missionary consistently chooses to have frightening "what if" thoughts about the bad things that will happen when speaking in public or being the center of attention, social anxiety will continue. Anytime any of us consistently make such choices, there is nothing that God can do to solve our problem without overruling our agency in the process.

It's also true that things we earn generally mean more to us than the things we are given; and we grow more by achieving goals on our own than we do when our desires are given to us. Obviously, there are many things we simply can't do on our own, or need direction when doing. Therein is the primary reason why we pray and depend so often on divine assistance. And some of the big ticket items in life, such as redemption and sanctification, are pure gifts from the Savior. Nevertheless, we can often do more for ourselves than we think. God often steps in when we truly can go no further on our own; not when we think we have reached our limit.

God will only do that which is in our best long-term interest; and in the best interest of His other children. God's promise that He will answer our prayers can be trusted absolutely; but the promise comes with fine print that needs to be remembered. As the Savior pointed out, "And whatsoever ye shall ask the Father in my name, *which is right, believing that ye shall receive,* behold it shall be given unto you" (3 Nephi 18:20, italics added). God may at times permit us to do foolish things when we insist; but He will never do for us or to us something that is not in our long-term best interest. Elder Richard G. Scott put it this way. "His invitation, 'Ask, and ye shall receive' (3 Nephi 27;29) does not assure that you will get what you *want*. It does guarantee that, if worthy, you will get what you *need*, as judged by a Father that loves you perfectly, who wants your eternal happiness even more than do you" (Richard G Scott, "Trust the Lord", *Ensign*, November, 1995).

The Savior himself faced this reality at the moment of His supreme sacrifice. His prayer was, "Oh my Father, if it be possible, let this cup pass from me; nevertheless, not as I will but as thou will" (Matthew 26:39). I'm sure that if there was any other way, it would have been preferred, both by the Father and the Son. But there was no other way; and so the Father allowed, and the Savior proceeded with what had to be done. The Father even allowed the Son to experience this ultimate test without his comfort and help. As He closed in on victory, the Savior was heard to cry, "My God, my God, why hast thou forsaken me?" (Matthew 27:46). Elder Jeffrey R. Holland in reflecting on this poignant moment made the following observations:

> "Indeed, it is my personal belief that in all of Christ's mortal ministry the Father may never have been closer to His son than in these agonizing final moments of suffering. Nevertheless, that the supreme sacrifice of His son might be as complete as it was voluntary and solitary, the Father briefly withdrew from Jesus the comfort of His Spirit, the support of His personal presence. It was required, indeed it was central to the significance of the Atonement, that this perfect Son who had never spoken ill nor done wrong nor touched an unclean thing had to know how the rest of humankind—us, all of us—would feel when we did commit such sins. For His Atonement to be infinite and eternal, He had to feel what it was like to die not only physically but spiritually, to sense what it was like to have the divine Spirit withdraw, leaving one feeling totally, abjectly, hopelessly alone" (Jeffrey R. Holland, "None Were With Him", *Ensign*, May, 2009).

It was necessary for the Savior to suffer as He did; and we will be forever grateful for His willingness to make that sacrifice.

Understanding and pondering this can provide some solace when we are required to continue carrying burdens for which we have sought relief. The Savior's experience can help us understand that when we pray for and expect miracles that don't happen, God is still there; and although it may not be obvious because of our limited understanding, there is a good reason our request has been denied, or seriously delayed. The challenge and test then becomes to make the best of it by proceeding in faith to do the best we can under the circumstances we face. Certainly the example of the Savior is a bright light to follow as we do so.

Prayers may not be answered in the time frame we are expecting. Virtually all missionaries are familiar with, and frequently quote, Moroni's promise given toward the end of the Book of Mormon: "if ye shall ask with a sincere heart, with real intent, having faith in Christ, he will manifest the truth of it unto you by the power of the Holy Ghost. And by the power of the Holy Ghost ye may know the truth of all things" (Moroni 10:4-5). Missionaries and investigators can rely on this promise of obtaining a witness when they meet the criteria specified. It should be noted, however, that there is no promise as to when the witness will come. At times, a witness is received immediately; but in other cases it takes a very long time. Not understanding this, Sister Green and other missionaries, have gotten unnecessarily frustrated when they, or their investigators, have failed to get the immediate answer expected.

As faithful and spiritually dynamic as he was, President David O. McKay followed the pattern of Moroni 10:4-5, but had to wait a very long time for the special witness he sought; and when it came, it came in a natural and not particularly dramatic way. "The

31

spiritual manifestation for which I had prayed as a boy in my teens came as a natural sequence to the performance of duty" (*Teachings of the Presidents of the Church: David O McKay*, 162-69). Elder Richard G. Scott also experienced this truth personally. "Once it took me over ten years to discover the answer to an extremely important matter for which I had prayed consistently and earnestly" ("To Learn and to Teach More Effectively, BYU Education Week Devotional, August, 2007). The fact that an answer to a heartfelt prayer is not immediately forthcoming is cause for patience, not cause for concern or doubt.

Unrealistic Expectation: Excitement in the work and enjoyment of my mission will grow over the course of my service.

In addition to the unrealistic expectations mentioned above, Sister Green thought something was wrong because she wasn't as excited about the work one year in as she had been earlier in her service. She expected to be even more enthused and excited as her mission progressed. In reality, she found it harder to motivate herself each day; and the work day ahead often looked routine. It was even difficult to get excited about special days; such as a day when an investigator was to be baptized. On those days, Sister Green was happy for the investigators, knowing as she did that they were doing the right thing; but it was a more ho-hum and not the "your joy will be full" (D & C 18:15) kind of experience she had expected. She needed to change this expectation as follows.

Emotional experiences (feelings) tend to be more intense when something is new; but not as much after prolonged experience. The truth is that anything, even something that is very

32

important to us, tends to be less exciting, and related emotions are less intense, as time goes on. For example, Sister Green had a very special boyfriend serving in another mission. This was a relatively new relationship before her mission and her feelings were intense then, and still were. But suppose that these two were now home from their missions, and had been married for twenty years. She would hopefully still have strong feelings of love for him; but it's likely that she wouldn't be as excited to see him, or think about him as passionately as she did early on. Ideally the excitement and enthusiasm would have been replaced by a more mature love involving shared experience, trust, comfort and commitment; but the emotional experience would be different.

This seems to be the natural progression of feelings in missionary service as well. Appreciation of a mission and the lessons learned will often grow over time. Home sickness subsides and there is a comfort level that typically grows as a mission progresses. But the day-to-day experience may be less exciting and motivation harder to come by over time. As discussed later, there are steps that can be taken to address this common problem; but the fact that this happens is not cause for alarm, or reason to believe that something is terribly wrong.

Unrealistic Expectation: I will grow to love the people that I serve.

Before her mission, Sister Green had heard any number of returned missionaries indicate how much they had grown to love the people in their mission. She also heard the same thing repeatedly in the testimony of other missionaries serving with her. Unfortunately, she didn't have the warm, loving feelings that these missionaries described. She had trouble having kind feelings for the members of the ward in which she served. As a general rule, they were not very good member missionaries; and they tended to be cliquish and did not readily accept new people. The general population in her mission was very secular and she had trouble accepting their attitudes and lifestyle choices. The negative feelings these conditions generated caused Sister Green to feel inadequate and contributed to her sense that she was a failure as a missionary. Sister Green, of course, was right in thinking that it is important for missionaries to love those they serve; and that love usually grows with time in service; but she was using the wrong definition of love. Sister Green benefitted by changing her definition as follows:

We love others by serving them and treating them well. We can do this even if we don't have warm, loving feelings for them. Sister Green demonstrated love for those she served by doing all within her power to bring them to Christ. She had a sincere concern for their welfare and she was willing to serve them in any way she could. She was willing to put her life on hold and to put her needs second for eighteen months, which was an impressive act of love in itself. The normal effort she put forth every day demonstrated love. By this definition, she did love the people she served, and that type of love had grown over her mission. It would be ideal, but it was not necessary to also have warm, loving feelings for them. Once she changed her definition of what it means to love others, she naturally felt better about herself and her service; but she also found that she was better able to forgive those who disappointed her. She discovered that doing a better job of forgiving others, and not feeling so guilty about not "loving" them; in turn, led to warmer feelings for those she served.

34

Changing her expectation about how she would feel about the people she served; and rethinking the other unrealistic expectations mentioned above, led to a much more enriching experience on her mission. The same will be true for any missionary with the same or similar unrealistic expectations. In summary, prospective and serving missionaries should remember that:

1. **Obedience and faith are necessary in order to have a successful mission; but they do not guarantee a large number of baptisms.**
2. **The primary goal of a mission is to invite as many people as possible to come to Christ. Whether or not those invited accept the invitation is beyond a missionary's control.**
3. **Missionaries can have the Spirit in their work, but they may not feel it at any given time.**
4. **Many missionaries, Church leaders, and other faithful members have questions about some aspect of Church policy or doctrine.**
5. **Doubts are natural and arise for good reasons, including the fact that mistakes have been made by Church leaders in the past; and many things have not yet been revealed.**
6. **There is no way to answer questions in a way that will be satisfying to all investigators.**
7. **Even when missionaries are adequately prepared and bring the Spirit to their teaching, investigators may not be in a position to benefit.**
8. **Even when engaged in the service of the Lord, inspiration will not always be provided.**

9. God will not do for us what we must do for ourselves.
10. God will only do that which is in our best interest, and which is also in the best interest of others.
11. Prayers may not be answered in the time frame we are expecting.
12. Emotional experiences (feelings) tend to be more intense when something is new; but not so much after prolonged experience.
13. We love others by serving them and treating them well. We can do this even if we don't have warm, loving feelings for them.

CHAPTER TWO

MISTAKE TWO: WORRYING ABOUT THINGS THAT CAN'T BE CONTROLLED

Like most of us, virtually all missionaries understand that it makes no sense to worry about things that they can't control. But also like most of us, missionaries often worry about such things anyway. For example, an Elder's girlfriend back home had quit writing consistently. He was making himself sick worrying that she had met someone else. Two sister missionaries baptized a recent convert who then returned to her former bad habits; plus she had just lost her job and had no place to live. These missionaries were losing sleep in worry about her. An investigator who was very excited to hear their message just told the missionaries that he didn't want them to come back. The Elders involved worried about the investigator; but they also worried that they might have done something wrong in their teaching; or perhaps failed him in some way. There is no end to what missionaries can worry about; and most of their concerns are beyond their control. Thankfully, there are things that can be done to curb such worry, starting with an opportunity unique to people of faith—especially missionaries.

Trust the Savior

In the Sermon on the Mount, the Savior makes an important promise that missionaries may at times overlook. "Come unto me, all ye that labor and are heavy laden, and I will give you rest. Take my yoke upon you, and learn of me; for I am meek and lowly in heart; and ye shall find rest unto your souls. For my yoke is easy, and my burden is light" (Matthew 11:28-30). It's apparent that the great majority of missionaries have taken on the yoke of Christ. They are not perfect; yet they are committed in their discipleship. They are serving more, studying more, and living a more righteous life than ever before. They are also typically burdened like never before. They have taken on more responsibility and feel more pressure than ever. In fact, their experience in many cases seems to contradict the promise of the Savior cited above. In spite of their having taken on His yoke, their burdens certainly have not been lightened.

When this contradiction occurs, it's usually because the missionary has not recognized, or at least not taken advantage of, the opportunity inherent in having the Savior as a partner. To explain, think of what it means to be yoked to Christ. A yoke, of course, is a harness or crosspiece that is fastened to the necks of two animals in a way that allows them to pull some burden together. When two animals are thus yoked, the strength of each is multiplied, even beyond what would be expected by simply adding the power of each animal. For example, it has been reported that a typical Belgian draft horse can pull 8,000 pounds. When harnessed together with another, the two together can pull 20,000 to 24,000 pounds--significantly more than the sum of what each horse could pull alone. But assume that one of the horses had infinite power, in which case, the pulling power of the normal horse attached to it would be multiplied infinitely. No burden would be too much to pull.

This means that when yoked to the Savior we cannot lose. As discussed in the previous chapter, the only things that are impossible with the Lord involve contradicting the principle of agency; or doing something that will ultimately hurt or not be in our best interest, or in the best interest of others. Herein lies the opportunity to not worry about things we can't control. Since the one we are yoked to does everything perfectly, and has all power, we can rest assured that whatever He is involved in will ultimately work to our advantage, as well as to the advantage of others we care about. If we are yoked to the Savior, we therefore need not worry about unfortunate present circumstances, or unwanted future possibilities. Thanks to the Atonement, after repentance, we also need not worry about our past mistakes. In short, as long as we are partnered with the Savior and doing our best to follow Him, we need not worry about or fear anything! Again, in the words of the Lord, "Wherefore, be of good cheer, and do not fear, for I the Lord am with you, and will stand by you..." (D&C 68:6. Understanding and remembering this could lighten a missionary's burdens dramatically. In terms of the worry examples given above, here's how this can work:

Elder worried about his girlfriend. Elder Stewart hadn't received "the letter" yet; but he strongly sensed it was coming. The girlfriend he had left at home had basically quit writing; and her infrequent emails had hinted about dating someone else. As a result, Elder Stewart was a mess. His thoughts rotated between thinking things like, "We are meant to be together; and I'll never find anyone else I can love as much as I love her"; to "This other guy must have something I don't"; to "I've got to know what's going on—I've got to get through to her and convince her to wait". The fact that countless other missionaries have been in the same spot didn't ease Elder Stewart's pain. What did help was to trust the One to whom he was yoked.

An early leader in the Church received instructions and promised blessings which no doubt also apply to Elder Stewart and others who are willing to sacrifice their personal comfort and desires in serving the Lord. Warren A. Cowdery was instructed to "devote his whole time to this high and holy calling, which I now give unto (you), seeking diligently the kingdom of heaven and its righteousness, and all things necessary shall be added thereunto; for the laborer is worthy of his hire" (D&C 106:3). Elder Stewart could bank on the fact that *if* being together with his girlfriend was as critical to his happiness as he imagined; the Lord, within the constraints of the principle of agency, certainly has the power to make that happen. If not, Elder Stewart can rest assured that what he needs to be happy and successful in life will be provided. As the story of Job in the Old Testament illustrates, even those who have lost everything in the service of the Lord end up with far more than they sacrificed. "...the Lord gave Job twice as much as he had before" (Job 42:10); "So the Lord blessed the latter end of Job more than his beginning" (Job 42:12). The laborer is indeed worthy of his hire.

Thankfully, Elder Stewart's misery didn't last long. Once he gave up constantly thinking about his girlfriend and focused on the work, the pain eased; or stated differently, his burden was lightened. He learned the truth of what President Hinckley taught, "The best antidote for worry I know is work" (Gordon B. Hinckley, "The Words of the Prophet: Put Your Shoulder to the Wheel", *New Era*, June, 2000). Worrisome thoughts were overwhelmed by his faith that God wanted him to be eternally happy and that everything he needed for that to happen was guaranteed so long as he did his part. Elder Stewart made this faith operational by following a simple strategy. When he noticed that he was thinking of his girlfriend, he repeated to himself the simple truth: "I don't like this. I miss Karen so much. But I have to believe that, with God's help, it's all going to work out". Then he made an effort to immediately change the focus of his thoughts to something positive about his missionary work and present circumstance. Naturally, thoughts of Karen frequently snuck back in; but when they did, Elder Stewart just repeated the process. Soon thoughts of Karen subsided and interest and fulfillment in his missionary work increased.

Sisters worried about the struggles of a recent convert. It's common for missionaries to develop a special bond with some of those they serve; and to be very concerned when these individuals have significant problems. Of course, the same is true when family and friends at home face serious challenges. Concern and caring are a part of any close relationship; but an unnecessary burden is created when a missionary moves beyond caring and takes on the responsibility to solve the problems of those they care about. The Sisters mentioned above naturally wanted to do everything within their power to help their friend; but they quickly reached the limit of their ability to help. They had prayed for their friend. They had alerted the Bishop and Relief Society President to the problem. They had visited their friend and showed their love and support. At that point, the only reasonable strategy was for them to turn the situation over to a higher power. The fact of being yoked with the Savior meant that they didn't have to look very far for that higher power.

Early leaders of the Church, Sydney Rigdon and Joseph Smith, were reminded of this in a way that I'm sure also applies to modern-day servants of the Lord. "Verily, thus saith the Lord unto

41

you, my friends Sidney and Joseph, your families are well; they are in mine hands, and I will do with them as seemeth me good; for in me there is all power" (D&C 100:1). Joseph and Sydney were no doubt reminded of this comforting truth in order to help them avoid unnecessary worry and concern. The same blessing is available to these two sister missionaries, or any of us for that matter, if we will turn concern about all things beyond our control over to God. As the Apostle Peter directed: "Humble yourselves therefore under the mighty hand of God, that he may exalt you in due time; Casting all your care upon him; for he careth for you" (1 Peter 5:6-7). Or as we read in Psalms: "Cast thy burden upon the Lord, and he shall sustain thee; he shall never suffer the righteous to be moved" (Psalm 55:22).

Of course, realizing this blessing depends on our having faith in the Lord's infinite love and power; and even more importantly, in His wisdom. As discussed in the previous chapter, faith in His wisdom is needed when the Lord doesn't act as quickly, or in the manner that we think is necessary. Perhaps part of the reason this happens at times lies in the fact of our limited perspective. As mortals, we tend to "catastrophize" problems. Many of the things in life that happen are horrible, awful, and totally unacceptable from our perspective. But if we could see the end from the beginning; or in other words, if we were able to see present calamity in an eternal perspective, the horrible things that happen might look a little different. As an analogy, think of a young child with a bad toothache. Let's say that he has been traumatized by previous trips to the dentist. Imagine him screaming and pleading with his mother to not take him to the dentist again. Hopefully this mother will take him anyway, even with him screaming for relief. Why? Because she sees what her son does not. The trip to the dentist is necessary in order to remove the pain and to avoid a bigger problem later.

From a mortal perspective, their friend faced a horrible situation; but the problem may not have looked as bleak from God's perspective. In any event, because of His infinite love for their friend, and the fact that He has the power to do for her what needs to be done; these sisters could safely leave their friend's problems in His hands. They would then continue to care; but they would no longer feel responsible or desperate about the situation. Thus their burden would be greatly lightened.

Missionaries are told by a promising investigator to not come back. When this happens, as it will inevitably at some point in a mission, worry about the investigator and his future can be eliminated by turning the problem over to the Lord, as just discussed. There is also a further advantage of being yoked to the Savior. It can allow missionaries to quit feeling guilty and concerned that they might have dropped the ball with their investigator in some way.

Elder Ling and Elder Gordon had this opportunity with one of their investigators. They met Grant under an unusual circumstance. They arrived for an appointment with his next door neighbor only to find no one home. At that point, even though it was getting late and they couldn't see a light on in the neighboring house, they felt impressed to knock on Grant's door. To their pleasant surprise, he was home and received them warmly. He told the Elders that he normally had no use for those who came knocking on his door unsolicited; but for some reason he felt like he should invite them in. A series of discussions ensued and Grant was very interested in the Elder's message. He began reading the Book of Mormon and he attended Church. Then out of the blue, and with no real explanation, Grant told the Elders that he was no longer interested and he didn't want them to contact him again.

Along with concern about Grant, this disappointing outcome led to worry that they might have done something to offend him. They wondered if they had pushed him too much; or maybe they hadn't been sufficiently direct. Maybe they didn't answer his questions adequately, or they might have chosen the wrong sequence of topics in their teaching. They picked apart their efforts with Grant, assuming that they must have done something wrong. Of course, there is wisdom in missionaries reviewing their teaching methods and evaluating how well they are doing (see PMG, p. 21). This, however, works best if done under inspiration and without being overly critical. The Lord will bless us with information about our weakness (Ether 12:27), but in a way and at a time that will help us become stronger. Satan will beat us over the head with our weaknesses in an attempt to discourage and overwhelm us. That was essentially what was happening to these two Elders.

The fact is that, however imperfect their effort, both Elder Ling and Elder Gordon had pulled their share of the load. They cared about Grant and had done their best to invite him to see the truth. They had prayed sincerely for him. They planned their lessons prayerfully; and they followed the recommendations in Preach My Gospel. They had also made efforts to get members of the ward involved with Grant. Having done everything within their power, they could rely on the Lord to do the rest. They could rely on the fact that everything that needed to be done beyond their limited ability would be done. Understanding and accepting this truth would have lightened the burden of these Elders considerably.

How Do We Know When We Are Pulling Our Share of the Load?

Unfortunately, it didn't work out that way for Elders Ling and Gordon, primarily because they had a hard time believing that they had actually pulled their share of the load. This doubt resulted in part from making the common mistake of assuming that since their efforts failed to produce the result they sought, they must have done something wrong. Then in hindsight, they thought of many things they could have done differently, which supported the hypothesis that they had failed in some way.   For instance, these Elders could have followed a different plan in teaching Gordon that *might* have been more effective. After the fact, they thought of pertinent scriptures that they didn't think of at the time; and they came up with better answers to some of Gordon's questions that m*ight* have made a difference.

The key word here, however, is "might". There is no way for them to know for sure if anything they *might* have done differently would have made a difference. But the Lord knows; and He was their partner in the teaching effort. Given that they were yoked to the Savior, if there was something they could have done differently that would have made all the difference, it's safe to assume that they would have been inspired to know what that was at the time. Since that didn't happen; these Elders had good reason to assume that they had done what needed to be done. No matter what else they *might* have done, it would not have made a difference. Sadly, instead of following this logic, they assumed that they must have done something wrong, thus experiencing unnecessary worry and guilt.

Another reason Elders Ling and Gordon had a hard time believing that they had given their best effort had to do with the fact that important principles involved in missionary service, such as faith, preparation and obedience, are open-ended and hard to define. Missionaries are continually taught the truth that success in their work requires faith. It requires adequate preparation, and missionaries must be obedient to receive the blessings they seek (D&C 4: D&C 130:20). But at what point is faith, preparation, or obedience sufficient? These are open ended concepts which means that there is no way we can ever do all that is possible. It seems like we mortals could always have more faith; and there is no obvious end to the study and preparation that we could make when working toward important goals. There are also always shades of gray in definitions and our inevitable human imperfections which make exact obedience technically impossible.

As examples of these issues, in spite of their desire and considerable faith, there were still times when these Elders had doubts that specific prayers would be answered; and they had trouble at times having confidence in the inspiration they received. Their minds sometimes wandered during their study, and circumstances came up that resulted in hurried planning sessions on occasion. In spite of their best intentions, there were times when they were a few minutes late getting out of their apartment in the morning, or they failed to keep missionary rules in some other minor way. But such is life for even the best missionaries. Elders Ling and Gordon consistently made dedicated effort to build their faith. They did their best to make study and preparation effective, and they followed mission rules and general commandments to the best of their understanding and ability. By any reasonable standard, in spite of their imperfections, they were doing the best they could.

At least they were doing the best they could under the circumstance of being human. As suggested above, and discussed in detail in later chapters, none of us can be perfect in this life (see Russell M. Nelson, "Perfection Pending", October General Conference, 1995). But we can be perfect sometimes, in some things. For instance, there were times when Elder Ling's personal study sessions were wonderfully illuminating and inspiring. The fact that he knew from experience that it was possible, led Elder Ling to believe that all sessions should be like that. Unfortunately, there were inevitably other times when he didn't feel well, when he was tired or distracted; or when that perfect experience didn't happen for any number of reasons. Those were times when he needed to do what he could to get back on track, and to persevere in giving it his best effort; but he also needed to accept the fact that his best effort was effected by factors in his current circumstance; and those factors were often largely beyond his control.

The fact is that missionaries are successful when they give their best effort to be obedient, live righteously, and help others live the gospel (PMG, p. 11). However, when defining "best effort", the circumstances a missionary faces must be considered. As just described, because of human limitations, the best effort of a missionary will vary at different times due to circumstances over which a missionary has little control. Likewise, because of differing abilities and experience, the best effort in the case of one missionary will not be the same as it will be for another. The good news is that a missionary's partner, when he or she is yoked to Christ, is perfect at all times, in all ways, and under all circumstances. In short, missionaries who are doing their best under the circumstances don't have to be perfect in their service. They can always trust the Lord to do what needs to be done when their best efforts fall short.

It's also comforting to remember that the Lord understands our human condition and will judge and bless us accordingly. For example, when we partake of the Sacrament we do not promise to keep the commandments; but rather we covenant that we are *willing* to do so (D&C 20:77). Also as we read in the Doctrine and Covenants, we get points for trying. "For verily I say unto you, they are given for the benefit of those who love me and keep all my commandments, *and him that seeketh so to do*" (D&C 46:9, italics added). Again from the Doctrine and Covenants, "For I, the Lord, will judge all men according to their works, *according to the desire of their hearts*" (D&C 137:9, italics added). The Lord apparently understands that the best we can do will often not be perfect; but He will still bless us as long as we desire to do what's right, and are doing our best to make that happen.

As a practical matter, when deciding whether you are doing the best you can under the circumstances, consider the following rule of thumb:

You know you have done your best when you are committed and prayerful, but can't think of anything you can do to solve a problem, other than what you have already been doing. In which case, it makes sense

to keep hopeful, to keep committed; and to be open to new ideas that might come along. At the same time, you can rest assured that you are doing the best you can.

When God is our partner, our prayers will be heard and answered; which means that if there is something else we need to do in order to solve a problem, it will be made known to us. A loving Father wouldn't make us guess and then condemn us for not coming up with the right answer. And when we are doing, or have done, the best we can to solve a problem that persists, then that problem is obviously beyond our control. As described in the next section, all such problems can be turned over to the Lord.

A Practical Suggestion Regarding How to Overcome Worry

It's easy to see the virtue in refusing to worry about things that we can't control. But most of us realize that this is one of many things in life that is easier said than done. Fortunately, as described in some detail above, we have been given the wonderful invitation to yoke ourselves to the Savior. When we do that, we can trust Him to do for us and our loved ones what we can't. We can then trust that no matter how bleak our present or immediate future might be, God is with us and all things will work to our ultimate advantage. This truth provides a solid philosophical foundation as we attempt to avoid unnecessary worry.

As important as this philosophical foundation is, however, it's also important to have a practical strategy by which this philosophical principle can be applied. In that regard, you might find the following exercise helpful. This exercise was instrumental in Sister Bouchet finally getting a handle on her habit of overwhelming worry.

49

Sister Bouchet had always been a worrier, but nothing like she had become while on her mission. She worried about her investigators, her companion, pending transfers, and her performance as a missionary. She worried about her teaching skills, problems at home, her health, her weight; and she had countless other concerns. Following are the steps she took to help manage this problem.

Step One: Sister Bouchet made a list of all her worries, placing these worries under three headings. The headings were 1) Worries that I can do something about; 2) Worries that I can't do anything about; and 3) Worries that I'm not sure whether I can do anything about or not. She completed this list by taking about ten minutes in one individual study session to start the list, then a few minutes in two subsequent sessions to add any additional ideas that came to mind. As was true of all her study sessions, she began this effort with a prayer for inspiration and guidance.

Step Two: Sister Bouchet took a few minutes in additional study sessions to focus on the worries that she had recorded in the "I can do something about" category. She wrote down all of the practical things that came to mind that would address each of these worries. She then took out her planner and scheduled a time to do the things that she had identified, along with a pledge to herself that she would follow through with the planned action. Then when she was tempted to worry about one of these concerns at an unscheduled time, she reminded herself not to worry about it. She would worry about the issue only at the time and in the way designated in her planner. She didn't have to deal with it at that moment.

Step Three: Sister Bouchet drew a big X through the many items on her list that she knew she couldn't do anything about. Going forward, when these worries popped into her head, she reminded herself that there was nothing further she could do about the problem, other than leave the issue in the hands of God. She then tried immediately to change the focus of her thoughts to something positive in her missionary work or current situation. She didn't try to convince herself that there was nothing to worry about; or that everything would be OK. She simply tried to get her mind off of the worry altogether. Otherwise, by trying to convince herself that she didn't need to worry, she would still be thinking about the issue, which could eventually end up fueling her worry. She also tried to be patient and not worry about the fact that it took time to get good at changing the focus in her mind. At first, the worry that she was trying to rid herself of tended to came back within a few seconds or minutes of her trying to change the subject in her head. With persistent effort, however, she was able to get past a compelling worry much quicker; and eventually it became a non-issue.

Step Four. For those worries that she didn't know whether she could do anything about or not, Sister Bouchet sought outside advice. Naturally she sought divine help in determining if there was anything she could do to help solve the problem; but she also sought advice from others she trusted. During one of her scheduled interviews, she mentioned one or two of the worries in this category to her Mission President, and asked if he could see anything she could do about it that she hadn't considered.   She sent an email to a trusted older sister at home asking for her opinion about an item or two on the list. Also, Sister Bouchet did some brainstorming with her companion regarding what might be done to help resolve some the problems she worried about. The goal was to move all of the worries she was uncertain about into one of the first two categories. If any of her outside resources suggested practical things she could do to solve the problem, she then moved the worry into the first category—Worries I can do something about—and made an appropriate plan to do what she could to resolve it. If not, she moved it into the second category—Worries about which there is nothing I can do. The goal was then, of course, to eliminate the worry about those items, as in Step Three.

After a few weeks of conscious effort as described above, Sister Bouchet noticed having fewer worries in general; and those remaining were constructive. She only worried about things she could do something about; and those worries felt more positive because she had a plan to do her part to resolve the issue. As expected, the result was that she became a much less tense, happier, and more effective missionary. She also noticed a significant improvement in her health. The previous constant worry had added a great deal of stress lowering her immune system and causing headaches and gastro-intestinal problems.

Since Sister Bouchet's worries are common to many missionaries, specifics might be helpful. Below is a representative list of some of the worries that she had, along with a summary description of what she decided to do about them.

Worries that she could do something about. Sister Bouchet had two items in this category—her recent weight gain and the fact that she worried too much. With respect to her weight, Sister Bouchet identified several factors that were contributing to her weight gain. For one, she and her companion too often took the easy way out and indulged in fast food. Given their circumstance, it was also hard for them to manage their intake when eating with members or investigators. The culture in which they served tended to force feed missionaries and put a lot of pressure on them when they declined large portions and/or second helpings. A third obvious problem was a lack of exercise. She and her companion usually found a reason to skip their morning exercise, and now that they had a car, they no longer got much exercise at all. To cap it off, Sister Bouchet's companion was from the local culture and had little interest in helping her address these issues. In fact, she didn't understand Sister Bouchet's concern about her weight and accused her of vanity.

In spite of how difficult these factors were to deal with, it was clear to Sister Bouchet that her weight was a problem within her control. With a little thought and prayerful consideration, Sister Bouchet came up with a list of things she could do to help stabilize her weight. She then formalized these ideas and established a specific, written plan with dates and check-in points for the various elements of the plan. She also shared the problem with her mother who sent a little extra money to fund the purchase of healthy snacks; which was a part of the plan that required outside help. As expected, there were complications and she found it difficult to implement her plan; but with perseverance and a few changes to her approach, she was able to see significant improvement, even with her current companion. Then when she eventually got a new companion who was equally concerned about weight and health, the success was complete.

In the meantime, the challenge was to not worry about her weight so much. She discovered that worry about it was actually one of the factors contributing to the problem. Her constant worry and focus on food actually increased her appetite; while also lowering the level of self-control she was able to exert. Developing patience with her situation and learning not to worry about her weight proved to be her biggest challenge; which is generally true in the case of a classic worrier like Sister Bouchet.

So what did she do about her worry habit? Completing the exercise described above was an important first step in this process. Doing so sensitized her to the problem and provided a means for controlling her worry. In this regard, Step Three above proved to be especially helpful. As described above, Step Three involves a simple thought stopping technique that can be described as ADD. No, this does not mean Attention Deficit Disorder. The acronym, as used here, stands for (A) attention, (D) decision and (D) distraction. When she became aware A) of worry about her weight, she immediately made a decision (D) to not go there in her thinking. Following through with that decision was aided by remembering that she had a plan and she need not worry about the problem beyond doing her best to stick to the plan. Once she was aware of unproductive worry and had made the decision to stop it, she then made a conscious effort to distract (D) her thinking by changing the focus of her thoughts to something totally unrelated to her weight problem. Finally, she repeated this process over and over as often as needed whenever she noticed that her mind had reverted back to thoughts she didn't want.

Sister Bouchet also asked her Mission President to provide a referral to the Mental Health Advisor serving her area. Two or three visits by telephone proved to be helpful in understanding why she was such a worrier; and the counselling sessions helped her develop and follow through with specific strategies to overcome her bad habit.

Worries that were beyond her control. Sister Bouchet discovered that most things she worried about were beyond her control. The following four criteria helped her decide when a worry was in this category.

1. All worries that involved things that are a natural part of life, such as her father's cancer, were beyond her control.

2. Things that hadn't happened yet; and for which there was nothing practical she could do about it at the moment, were beyond her control. Examples included where and when she would be transferred next, and whether to go to school or work after returning from her mission.

3. Things that essentially involved the agency of others were beyond her control. Sister Bouchet had a long list of such worries; including her companion's problems, decisions made by her younger sister, her family's financial problems, decisions made by her boyfriend, problems in the Branch to which she was assigned, choices made by investigators, and her parent's marriage difficulties.

4. Things were beyond her control when she had carefully considered what she could do to solve a problem, but could think of nothing practical that

she could do about it. This was ultimately true of all items on her worry list, except those in the first category.

Sister Bouchet also found advice in her *Adjusting to Missionary Life* resource booklet to be quite helpful. "The past, the agency of others, the rules, the weather, government bureaucracies, the culture, your limitations, or the personality of other missionaries are outside of your control. Focus on things you can do something about, such as your behavior, your part of a relationship, your current choices, and your attitude" (*Adjusting to Missionary Life*, p. 31).

Worries that Sister Bouchet didn't know whether she could control or not. Sister Bouchet had four items on her list. (1) She worried about the fact that she and her companion had few progressing investigators. (2) She worried because she didn't get along well with her companion. (3) She was concerned because she wasn't enjoying her mission as much as she had expected. (4) She also worried about her health. She was experiencing more than the usual headaches and stomach problems.

Regarding the first issue of not having many progressing investigators, Sister Bouchet and her companion had sincerely prayed about the problem and they were doing everything they could think of to resolve it. Still, it felt like there must be more they could do. They therefore asked for help from others they trusted. They began by asking their Sister Training Leaders to spend some time with them, specifically designed to evaluate their approach and to identify anything that they could do differently. They also made it a point to ask for specific suggestions during

District and Zone meetings. When they had an opportunity to visit with their Mission President or his wife, they also asked for their advice. They followed through on any suggestions received; but still were not having much success. Given this effort, these Sisters decided that they were doing everything they could to solve the problem. They determined therefore to continue serving faithfully; while also remaining open to new ideas and approaches that might come along. But in the meantime, they decided not to worry about the problem. Whenever they were tempted to again worry or feel guilty about the lack of progressing investigators, they employed the ADD strategy outlined above.

Problems getting along with her companion, and trouble enjoying her mission were two additional worries that Sister Bouchet was not certain whether or not she could do anything about. She understood that her companion's problems were beyond her control; and those worries had already been moved to the "can-do-nothing about" list. However, there was still the possibility that she herself could do something to improve the relationship with her companion. She just didn't know what that might be. Again, she sought advice from those she trusts. In this case, she sought out her Mission President's wife, as well as the Mental Health Advisor, for their help. They actually did offer advice that Sister Bouchet found to be helpful. She therefore, moved this issue to the list of worries that she could do something about; and made a specific plan to work on it.

Likewise, she didn't know what she could do to enjoy her mission more than she did; and again she sought advice from the Mission President's wife and the Area Mental Health Advisor. Through their advice she discovered that the biggest thing she could do to enjoy her mission more was to overcome unnecessary worry and guilt. Since that was already a main item on her to-do list, there was no reason to worry about it beyond what she was already committed to do. It should be noted that once Sister Bouchet made progress avoiding unnecessary worry, she did begin to truly enjoy her mission. She was able to be herself more often, and she smiled more and laughed more. Generally, she had a whole lot more fun in her calling.

Lastly, Sister Bouchet was concerned about her health problems. She had frequent headaches and stomach problems that were limiting her missionary service. Her relatively poor health was also lowering the quality of her missionary experience. She often prayed for relief, and she had received priesthood blessings. At her Mission President's suggestion, she was examined by a physician, who found no significant physical health problem. She also consulted with the Area Mental Health Advisor regarding the possibility of an emotional component to her health concerns. Given all of this, there really wasn't anything else she could do. Therefore, this too was a problem that needed to be moved to the "can-do-nothing-about" category. Not surprisingly, she found that her health improved significantly once she had better control over her tendency to worry.

A Suggestion from the Savior Regarding Worry.

As an additional thought on the problem of worry about things over which a missionary has no control, consider the Savior's invitation to all of us: "Peace I leave with you, my peace I give unto you...Let not your heart be troubled, neither let it be afraid" (John 14:27).

Amazingly, this blessing and instruction was given on the very night of Gethsemane; at the beginning of what He knew would be His infinite suffering on behalf of all mankind. The fact that the Lord was talking about peace at a time like that, and encouraging His followers to not be afraid, is evidence of His great courage; and also of His ability to find peace in a situation that would give most of us fits of worry. This comment is also an invitation to not be afraid or worry about whatever might distress us in our lives. But as Elder Jeffry R. Holland has suggested, this may be more than just an invitation. He suggests that this might better be thought of as a commandment; and that it offends God when we break this commandment by letting our hearts be troubled. Said Elder Holland:

> "I can tell you this as a parent: as concerned as I would be if somewhere in their lives one of my children were seriously troubled or unhappy or disobedient, nevertheless I would be infinitely more devastated if I felt that at such a time that child could not trust me to help or thought his or her interest was unimportant to me or felt unsafe in my care. In that same spirit, I am convinced that none of us can appreciate how deeply it wounds the loving heart of the Savior of the world when he finds that his people do not feel confident in his care or secure in his hands or trust in his commandments" ("Come unto Me", *Ensign*, April 1998).

Given Elder Holland's perspective, Sister Bouchet and other chronic worriers may have something else to worry about. Not only is excessive worry unhealthy, it may be offensive to God. Missionaries stuck in unnecessary worry might find this thought motivating as they attempt to follow Sister Bouchet's example by overcoming this debilitating habit.

CHAPTER THREE

MISTAKE THREE: THINKING AND SPEAKING IN ABSOLUTES

Who says that missionaries don't swear? One morning as they were preparing to leave their flat, two Sister missionaries had a heated argument that started out something like this:

Sister A. I gave you the car keys. Where are they?

Sister B. No you didn't! I don't have them.

Sister A. You're kidding right! I know you have them somewhere. Look at your side of the room. You couldn't find anything in that mess!

Sister B. You're always blaming me for everything; and I'm sick and tired of it. And just because you are a neat-freak doesn't mean I have to be.

Thus began an argument that branched out from initial accusations to other issues, resulting in hurt feelings, a damaged relationship, and loss of the Spirit. Things got so bad that these two Sisters decided that they couldn't go out to work in their frame of mind; and they lost most of a day before they were able to settle their differences sufficiently to work together. And even after working through the immediate anger and hurt, their relationship remained strained for some time. It's interesting to note that through all of their heated exchange, neither Sister used foul language; something they seldom if ever did. Even so, they were indeed swearing at each other, at least in the biblical sense.

Swearing in the biblical sense means to make absolute, argumentative statements about something. Here is what the Savior said in the Sermon on the Mount about this kind of swearing:

> "Again, ye have heard that it hath been said by them of old time, Thou shalt not forswear thyself, but shalt perform unto the Lord thine oaths:
>
> But I say unto you, Swear not at all; neither by heaven; for it is God's throne;
>
> Nor by the earth; for it is his footstool; neither by Jerusalem; for it is the city of the great King.
>
> Neither shalt thou swear by thy head, because thou canst not make one hair white or black.
>
> But let your communication be, Yea, yea; Nay, nay: for whatsoever is more than these cometh of evil" (Matthew 5:33-37).

In this counsel from the Master, we are advised to avoid swearing to the truth of something, and to be neutral (yea, yea and nay, nay) in our communication with others. But what does that mean exactly? As suggested above, the Lord isn't talking about profanity, which most Latter-day Saints find offensive and try to avoid. Nor is he suggesting that we be wishy-washy in our faith and beliefs. That would contradict other direction found in scripture; such as, "I know thy works, that thou art neither cold nor hot: I would thou wert cold or hot. So then because thou art lukewarm and neither cold nor hot, I will spue thee out of my mouth" (Revelation 3:15-16). More likely, God is giving us some very practical advice in this scripture; which, if followed, would certainly have blessed Sisters A and B.

The Lord begins in the Matthew verses by warning against committing perjury (forswearing). We are reminded that under the Law of Moses it was forbidden to perjure oneself, especially in covenants made with God. Both a clear conscience, and a society that functions well, require honesty in our oath making. After confirming this basic doctrine, the Lord then teaches a higher law. Absolute statements about the truth of things--in effect, swearing to the truth of something in our everyday conversations--are also to be avoided.

Sister A was swearing when she made the emphatic point that her companion definitely had the car keys. Sister B responded by swearing that she did not. Each Sister was absolutely convinced that she was right; however, given human imperfection in perception and memory, it's possible that they might have been mistaken. In fact, one of these Sisters was obviously wrong; or perhaps both of them were. Someone else might have taken the keys, or perhaps they were still in the car somewhere.

As often happens, when Sister A's emphatic statement about the keys was denied with equal emphasis, she became argumentative, pointing out how messy her companion was. This attack, elicited a defensive and argumentative response about how

63

picky Sister A was. From there, around and around they went, getting more and more hurtful with each round.

Their argument and ensuing hard feelings could have been easily avoided if they had followed the savior's advice. Putting this in practical terms, instead of swearing that they definitely knew what had happened, they might have said something similar to, "You might be right" or "Maybe so". In other words, if each Sister had simply admitted that she might be wrong, even if she was convinced otherwise, it would have made all the difference. Almost like magic, contention would have disappeared from this experience. The conversation would then have gone something more like:

Sister A. I gave you the car keys. Where are they?

Sister B. Maybe you did, but I don't think so. Are you sure?

Sister A. Well yah, I remember handing them to you when we got out of the car; but I could be wrong about that.

By simply not swearing, these Sisters could have avoided the argument about who is too messy and who is too much a neat-freak; plus all the other accusations they ended up hurling at each other. Rather than spending time attacking and defending, they would likely have turned their attention to finding the keys and getting on with their day. In the process, they would obviously have saved their companionship and themselves a lot of grief.

It should be noted that in following the Savior's direction, these Sisters didn't have to agree with the other's point of view, or go along with anything that contradicted their values. All that was required is that they respect each other's opinion, even when they believed the other to be wrong. This rule was important in the situation these Sisters faced; but it's also a general rule applicable even when the issue is a matter of faith, or something of great importance. Suppose, for example, that in their conversations later in the day, someone claimed that Joseph Smith was a charlatan, certainly not a prophet. Rather than counter by making an emphatic statement such as, "Oh yes he was!"; it would be better to say something less confrontational, such as, "I can see why you might feel that way, but let me tell you why I know that he was a prophet"--followed by bearing a simple testimony. This approach would obviously be better from the standpoint of interpersonal relationships; but it would also make a more powerful case for the truth.

Additional Scripture Supporting This Approach.

Another scripture from the Sermon on the Mount is also relevant to the discussion here. In fact, it gives direction on what to do in place of swearing.

> "Agree with thine adversary quickly while thou art in the way with him, lest at any time he shall get thee, and thou shalt be cast into prison.
>
> Verily, verily, I say unto thee, thou shalt by no means come out thence, until thou hast paid the uttermost senine. And while ye are in prison can ye pay even one senine? Verily, verily, I say unto you, Nay" (3 Nephi 12:25-26). (Also compare Matthew 5:25-26. Note the interesting differences in the two renderings.)

Magic phrases such as "you might be right", or "maybe so" seem to fit nicely with the instruction to "Agree with thine adversary quickly". Saying it one more time, this can be done without compromising values or changing our belief. It's simply a matter of being agreeable rather than confrontational; and of respecting other points of view rather than trying to prove them wrong.

The exact reference intended in the above scripture about being cast into prison is less clear; although the impact being disagreeable has on relationships certainly applies. When we are negative and contradictory with others, our relationships with them suffer. The person whose feelings have been hurt by our actions is likely to lock us out (like we are in prison). And while we are locked out, sometimes our best effort to make amends and improve things is stymied or ineffective ("can ye pay even one senine?"). Finally, it will generally take considerable effort to get back in the other's good grace and reestablish the relationship ("paid the uttermost senine").

In the case of Sisters A and B, once they had offended each other sufficiently, a wall went up between them. Trust was lost, which meant that even attempts to apologize were met with deaf ears. It took considerable time and effort to get back to where they accepted and trusted each other. And even then, their relationship was on thin ice for some time, vulnerable to minor problems that would break through the ice and drown their relationship once again.

It was certainly true in the case of these two Sisters; but think how much relationships with others, in general, would improve if we never swore, and if the opinions of others were always respected. Good communication requires it. Nothing shuts down communication quicker than being contradicted or relating to someone who is totally closed minded. If this happens when missionaries are working with local leaders, ideas do not get processed adequately and the missionary's relationship with local members will suffer. As illustrated above, when it happens in companionships, arguments occur and/or feelings get bottled up. Companions begin to feel misunderstood, disrespected and unloved. Along with losing the Spirit in their work, trust and feeling safe in the companionship becomes impossible. When this happens with investigators, the Spirit is likewise lost and the opportunity to bring them to Christ is compromised.

One's relationship with God also suffers when the advice in Matthew is not followed. Someone convinced that he is right about something will not be open to spiritual guidance. Even a very dramatic experience like that had by Alma (Alma 36:6-11) and Paul (Acts 9:4-19) may not convince a closed minded person of his error. For example, Laman and Lemuel were rebuked by an angel, but still there was no lasting change of heart (1 Nephi 3-31).

Practical Application

The scriptural imperative to avoid swearing to the truth of things and to be agreeable with our enemies is relevant in many everyday missionary experiences. Missionaries will have a problem whenever they do any of the following:

1. *Correct others when they get their facts wrong.* Unless the issue involves a substantial error that will make a

difference in someone's life, who cares? In the spirit of the scriptures cited above, let it go. For example, maybe your companion, at least in your understanding, misremembers the score of a ball game, or what you had for dinner the other day. Perhaps it seems to you that he or she is exaggerating a point, or is claiming something to be fact that you believe to be fantasy. In all cases, unless it is an issue that will have a significant impact on someone's life, there is no need to correct the comment. And even when you do decide that it's important to correct someone else, it usually helps to add the possibility that you could be wrong. For instance, "Maybe I have it wrong, but I thought _____".

2. *Immediately dismiss ideas or opinions voiced by others that seem foolish to you.* A look or comment that suggests that you think another's statement or opinion is nonsense never wins points. The nonsense might make sense from a different perspective. Even if it doesn't, everyone is entitled to their opinion. For instance, maybe your companion's interpretation of a mission rule seems ridiculous to you. Or perhaps he or she is very worried about something that you think is no big deal at all. In the spirit of the scriptures cited above, it's always best to respect the other's opinion in these situations, even when you don't agree with them; or when their ideas seem foolish to you.

3. *Make categorical, emphatic statements contradicting another.* We have all heard or even made contradicting

statements that cut off communication and demean others. Just a few examples include:

"No way!"

"You've got to be kidding!"

"That's ridiculous!"

"How could you say/believe that?"

"Come on, get real."

It's important also to keep in mind that non-verbal communication can have the same effect. Rolled eyes or a moan will often send a message that you think a comment is ridiculous as readily as saying the words.

4. *Not declaring; or conversely, demanding that our wishes be met*. Declaring preferences and beliefs is essential in missionary work and when functioning in leadership positions. In those situations, we want people to know where we stand and what's important to us. It's also often useful to express our preferences and wishes in routine social situations as well. For example, when a missionary asks his companion what he would like to do for P-day, it's often annoying to hear back, "I don't care." That places all of the responsibility for the decision on one person, which can be burdensome. Effective compromise and planning requires that all of those involved in a decision participate by sharing their opinion. On the other hand, it's important to avoid stating our preferences and wishes in a demanding way. For example, it's better to avoid statements, such as "we can't do that"; or "we have to do it this way". A preferred response is

something like, "I'm not comfortable with that, but let's talk about it". Or one might say, "That doesn't really work for me. Let's find something that will work for both of us".

5. *Use force language.* Stating things in absolute terms such as "have to", "must" or "need" conveys the idea of no choice in the matter, which is seldom true and usually offensive. Rather than making a demand, it's better to simply state what you would like. For example, rather than saying "We have to go see the Reynolds again today", it would work better to say "I feel strongly that we should visit with the Reynolds today." Rather than saying, "You always put me down"; it would be better to say, "It seems like you put me down a lot." More will be said about this general problem in the next section.

Do I Want to or Do I Have to?

Swearing to the truth of things as discussed above can create problems in relationships; and those problems can be extreme when missionary companions are required to spend every moment within sight and sound of each other. Thinking in absolutes, or using force language in our heads, can also cause problems for the individual missionary. As part of the problem with force language, thinking that we have to do something can cause motivation and enjoyment problems.

Suppose, for example, that someone puts a gun to my head and forces me to put thirty pounds on my back and walk twenty

70

miles. I would likely hate every step of the way. All of the natural aches and pains involved would be exaggerated and more deeply felt. However, if I chose to do the very same thing, as I have done a number of times over the years, it would be a very pleasant experience. The difference, of course, lies in wanting to do something versus thinking that we have to do it. We naturally resist compulsion and force, whether the compulsion is coming from an outside source or from within ourselves. And when we feel that we are forced to do something, it tends to take the fun out of it, even if it's something that we would otherwise enjoy.

This means that a missionary who chooses to serve a mission, and emphasizes that choice in his thinking, will have a more positive experience than one who thinks he has no choice. The truth is that no matter how much pressure from Church, family and friends, no one is forced to serve a mission. It is always a choice. Yet some missionaries keep thinking of their service in terms of something they have to do.

It works a lot better from an emotional standpoint if a missionary thinks, "This is hard, but I want to do this". During the difficult times, missionary work isn't naturally motivating; but there are still many good reasons why a missionary can honestly say that he wants to serve. For example, a committed disciple will want to do his duty, he wants to develop important life skills, he wants to give back for the blessings received, and his love of the Lord is motivating. Finding reasons such as these as to why he wants to do the hard thing; and then emphasizing those points in a way that allows him to honestly say that he wants to serve, can be motivating. Thinking of his mission as something that he has to do is demotivating and tends to make the experience painful.

Thinking in terms of "want to" not "have to" also makes it easier to get motivated to do specific things that can be difficult while serving a mission. For example, Elder Anderson's alarm goes off at 6:30am. If his first thought is "Oh no, I have to get up", he will have a harder time jumping out of bed than if he says to himself, "I want to get up". Again, he may not want to leave the comfort of the bed and face the day; but he can still want to get up because he wants to be obedient, he wants things to go smoothly during the day, he wants to have breakfast; or there can be any number of other positive reasons to do the otherwise negative thing. The truth is that Elder Anderson doesn't have to get up when the alarm goes off. Unfortunately, he has proven that to be true all too many times in the past. It will help him be more obedient if he quits thinking of getting up on time as a "have to" and emphasizes in his mind that this is something he really wants to do.

The important principle here is that how a missionary chooses to think about his service, and the specifics involved in that service, is an important factor in determining how he feels about what he is doing, and how motivated he is to do it. Feelings and motivation are the result of what we choose to think, not the other way around. For this reason, our feelings and motivation will change if our thinking changes. A missionary is therefore best served if he can remember that serving a mission is his choice; and there are good reasons why he wants to be where he is, doing all of the specific things he has been asked to do. As is always true, he is not forced to be obedient, but he can choose to be.

Do I Want it to Happen, or Do I Think it Needs to Happen?

Along with the problems indicated above, thinking that there is no choice—thinking that something needs to happen--will inevitably cause anxiety if the thing "needed" doesn't happen. As an example, I need to breathe. If someone chokes off my airways, I would quickly and understandably become anxious. Although the issues are not life-threatening, this will also happen when a missionary thinks that his girlfriend at home must wait for him, but he learns that she is engaged to someone else. It will happen when a missionary thinks that an investigator has to be baptized, but that investigator drops out of the teaching pool. Or it may be simply a matter of needing to be somewhere on time, but circumstances make it impossible to get there.

Again in these situations, it's much better to think in terms of "want to" and not "have to". Ideally, we want certain outcomes and will do everything within our power to make them happen. On the other hand, it is rarely the end of the world if what we want doesn't happen. Even if someone kept me from breathing and I died, that would be unfortunate at a number of levels; but thanks to the atonement, not a problem from an eternal perspective. The Elder who loses a girlfriend while serving will find a better one when he gets home. The investigator that missionaries care so much about will likely have other chances to see the truth. There is typically no earth shaking consequence if we are late getting to an appointment. These are all things that we want to happen and should do our best to make happen; but they are not actually needs. In fact, because of the Atonement, the only real need in this world is the need to have faith, and the need to do our best to be obedient to the commandments of God.

The problem is that when we think of anything as a need, whether it is an actual need or not, we will suffer emotionally when it doesn't happen. Therefore, since many things we want in this life don't happen; and since most everything that seems like a need really isn't, the only sensible thing is to get in the habit of thinking about most everything in our lives as a want and not a need. The process for making this change boils down to becoming aware of when we are thinking in absolutes. We can do this by listening to how we describe things to ourselves and others. When we hear "have to's", we can remind ourselves that the "need" is actually a want. We want something to happen; but it's not the end of the world if it doesn't.

As we try to do this, it may seem at first like we are fooling ourselves. Sure, we are telling ourselves that we don't really need whatever; but it will still feel very much like a need. When this process is repeated over time, however, the feeling of need will begin to go away.

Also, as we try to think this way, there may be some concern that by removing the sense of need, we will lose motivation to do hard things. The truth is we can still remain highly motivated to do our best to make what we want to happen actually happen. In fact, it can be more motivating when we focus on the reasons why the thing we want to do is important to us. Additional ideas on self-discipline and motivation to do hard things are offered in Chapter Ten.

Thinking in Absolutes is a Recipe for Frustration and Anger

Along with being demotivating, taking the fun out of things, and creating unnecessary anxiety, there is another problem with thinking in absolutes. Thinking in absolutes will often result in frustration and anger; and it may cause us to treat others improperly. Elder Lopez had a problem with his trainer who was overly picky and critical. Interestingly, this companion, Elder Davis, was overly critical primarily because he thought in absolutes. He realized that being so critical of his companion was not healthy; but he often felt like he had no choice. Essentially Elder Davis thought, "I don't like to be negative all the time, but as his trainer, I *have to* say something when my companion messes up." This wasn't true; but believing it, Elder Davis became overly critical, even when doing so went against his better judgement.

For his part, Elder Lopez also thought in absolutes. He would think things like: "He is *always* putting me down"; "I *can't* let him get away with it"; and "*I have to* stand up for myself". This isn't rocket science. It's easy to see that thinking this way would cause Elder Lopez to be angry with his companion; and it could eventually lead him to make inappropriate comments, or perhaps even become violent. That actually happened in the case of another missionary who kept thinking the way Elder Lopez was thinking. Eventually he had had enough and he said to his companion, "If you say one more thing I'm going to slug you". His companion said one more thing and he did slug him. Unfortunately, he landed a punch that did major damage, breaking his companion's jaw and sending him to the hospital.

75

This totally unacceptable and unfortunate incident happened primarily due to the fact that both companions involved in that incident, like Elders Lopez and Davis, kept thinking in absolutes. The basic Christian principles of patience, tolerance, and forgiveness all require that we think in a patient, tolerant and forgiving manner; i.e., that we not swear to ourselves or others. Using absolutes and force language when we describe things to ourselves is just the opposite. Elder Davis needed to think something more like, "To be a good Trainer, I don't have to comment on everything that I see Elder Lopez doing wrong. I will leave that for the really important things. Otherwise, loving my companion and accepting him is far more important than pointing out all of his faults". Elder Lopez would have been better off talking honestly with his companion about his frustration at being so frequently criticized; and then thinking something like, "I don't like this, but I can handle it". "However Elder Davis treats me, I'm going to take the higher road and follow the Savior's example".

Granted, thinking the way suggested for either Elder usually isn't natural, and it takes a bit of effort in real world situations. The benefits, however, are so great that it makes the effort worthwhile. Certainly, the tendency to be impatient, intolerant, and unforgiving is a big part of our natural man inclination. One of the blessings of missionary service is that it gives us so many opportunities to "put off the natural man"; which as we know, is a critical part of what we are here on earth to do (Mosiah 3:19).

It also seems like the tendency to focus more on what is wrong than what is right, is also a part of the "natural man" in all of us. Elders Davis and Lopez were both experiencing this problem. What his companion was doing wrong was obvious to Elder Davis; but the many good things were not as clear. Elder Lopez saw clearly the fact that Elder Davis was picky and overly critical; but he failed to recognize the many good qualities he had. This general problem is actually the fourth mistake that so many missionaries make; and is the subject of the next chapter.

CHAPTER FOUR

MISTAKE FOUR: FOCUSING ON THE NEGATIVE RATHER THAN THE POSITIVE

The fact is that our imperfect world is a composite of good and bad. As Lehi taught his son Jacob, "For it must needs be, that there is an opposition in all things" (2 Nephi 2:11). Along with all that is good, mistakes happen; people are imperfect; and evil exists alongside righteousness. As Lehi goes on to explain to Jacob, these negative elements are essential in a world designed to provide a unique learning environment; and a world in which we have the opportunity to be tested. The presence of both good and bad leaves us with a continuing series of choices in this life. Which will we choose? Where will our focus be?

Apostles and prophets throughout time have consistently warned us against evil choices in our behavior. The danger associated with such choices is obvious to anyone familiar with the scriptures; and to most of us through our own experience. Along with bad choices in what we choose to do, the Savior Himself (Matthew 5:27-30), and many apostles and prophets, have also warned us against evil choices in what we think. Bad choices in what we think include thoughts that are obviously evil; but also some thoughts that may not appear evil on the surface. These are typically choices that involve how we think about things in general—how we frame the world around us. The kinds of thoughts referred to here are primarily those that are negative and pessimistic. Such thoughts are not necessarily evil per se; but they will often lead to unproductive and evil outcomes. President Gordon B. Hinckley provides a warning about this type of thinking.

> "I am asking that we stop seeking out the storms and enjoy more fully the sunlight. I am suggesting that as we go through life we "accentuate the positive." I am asking that we look a little deeper for the good, that we still voices of insult and sarcasm, that we more generously compliment virtue and effort. I am not asking that all criticism be silenced. Growth comes of correction. Strength comes of repentance. Wise is the man who can acknowledge mistakes pointed out by others and change his course.

> What I am suggesting is that each of us turn from the negativism that so permeates our society and look for the remarkable good among those with whom we associate, that we speak of one another's virtues more than we speak of one another's faults, that optimism replace pessimism, that our faith exceed our fears. When I was a young man and was prone to speak critically, my father would say: 'Cynics do not contribute, skeptics do not create, doubters do not achieve'" (*Ensign,* Apr. 1986, 2–4).

This is particularly good advice for missionaries. The great majority of missionaries are protected from making purely evil choices by the requirements of their calling and their commitment. On the other hand, many are successfully tempted to be overly critical in what they think about themselves and others; and many succumb at times to the temptation to be cynical or pessimistic in general. It's interesting that such temptations may not look like temptation at first glance. Unhealthy self-criticism can masquerade as humility; or it can look like an effort to improve oneself. Unhealthy criticism of others can be excused as an effort to help them be better people. Cynicism and pessimism can be explained as just being honest; and optimistic thoughts can be described as naïve or a denial of realty.

No matter the motivation behind it, or the justification for it, a habit of focusing on the negative results in an unfortunate mindset that tends to color everything we see. Perhaps this is in part what the Savior was referring to in the Sermon on the Mount when He said, "the light of the body is the eye; if, therefore, thine eye be single, thy whole body shall be full of light. But if thine eye be evil, thy whole body shall be full of darkness. If, therefore, the light that is in thee be darkness, how great is that darkness" (3 Nephi 13:22-23). Among other interpretations, perhaps the Lord is pointing to the fact that if the focus of our perception and thoughts is primarily negative, if that's basically what we see when we look around us, our whole soul will be filled with darkness. Our confidence will suffer and peace of mind will be destroyed. If we focus on the positive, and are optimistic and upbeat in our thinking, our whole soul will be filled with light, thus increasing our confidence and bringing us closer to the Spirit.

Of course, having a positive mindset does not mean that we ignore the negative, just that we don't wallow in it, or end up overcome by it. Recognizing our weaknesses, when it fosters repentance and encourages hope and faith, is essential to healthy living. It's not such a good thing when it is overdone, leading to a loss of hope. Pointing out the mistakes of others can be a good thing too; but only on rare occasions, "when moved upon by the Holy Ghost" (D&C 121:43). It can be helpful only if done in a spirit of love and support. Recognizing negatives in a way that maintains hope and encourages change is much easier when we have developed the general habit of focusing on what's right and not what's wrong about ourselves and others. Stated metaphorically, we need to focus on the donut and not the hole.

Look at the Donut and Not the Hole

Two Sister missionaries were both experiencing firsthand how difficult a mission can be when you don't get along with your companion. When this happens, it's a great learning opportunity, but never much fun. Let's look at their situation first through Sister Richey's eyes. Her primary complaint was that her companion, Sister Patrick, was very quiet and passive. This forced Sister Richey to make most of the decisions and do most of the work. Worse, even though not being willing to make decisions herself, her companion was quick to criticize the decisions made by Sister Richey. Sister Patrick would typically not voice her criticism directly, but she made the point obvious non-verbally through body language. And whenever Sister Richey would ask what's wrong, Sister Patrick would say "nothing". She refused to discuss, or even admit, a problem. For these reasons, rather than being a confidante and support as many of her other companion's had been, Sister Patrick was a burden to Sister Richey.

All of this was a legitimate frustration. The good news is that Sister Richey was able to do two things that helped her deal with the problem. First, along the lines suggested in earlier chapters, she refused to accept responsibility for her companion's problems. At first, she was experiencing a lot of frustration, and she experienced a sense of failure, because her best efforts to change her companion weren't working. Once she decided that her companion's problems were beyond her control, and she gave up trying to fix them, much of that frustration was relieved. She didn't quit caring about her companion, or working on her part of the problem; she just quit feeling responsible to fix her companion's issues. This made it easier to continue to serve her companion by doing nice things for her; and she was better able to avoid verbally attacking her.

The second thing that helped was undertaking a campaign to see the good in her companion. As part of this campaign, Sister Richey made a list of her companion's strong points. At first this was a very short list. But with a little prayer and continued effort the list expanded considerably. As a sampling of her expanded list, she noticed that her companion had a strong testimony and understanding of the Book of Mormon and other scriptures. She was an avid reader and knew a lot about many things. She had a great relationship with her family and seemed well loved, especially by her nieces and nephews. In spite of the problems she had in their relationship, she didn't badmouth Sister Richey to others. She was a great cook and kept herself and their apartment clean. The list of these kinds of things that Sister Richey eventually came up with was extensive.

Sister Richey also made it a goal at the end of each day to think of three things that her companion had done well that day. Again, the negatives were dominant and tended to jump into her mind. In fact, before her campaign to be more positive, she spent a lot of time reviewing her companion's problems and how unfair the whole situation was. Now she made a determined effort to avoid dwelling on the obvious negatives and she searched for the positive. The good was there, she just hadn't seen it before. By seeing the good, and focusing on it, she was able to treat her companion more as Christ would. Sister Patrick continued to be quiet, passive, and negative through the remainder of their service together; but their relationship did improve somewhat and they were able to work effectively together most of the time. The biggest benefit of dwelling on the positive, however, came to Sister Richey herself. She became less frustrated and much better able to handle the difficult relationship. She became a happier and more productive missionary.

Now let's look at the companionship problem through Sister Patrick's eyes. In any relationship, there are always two sides to the story. Sister Patrick described her companion as being a driven perfectionist; one who didn't seem to be happy no matter what Sister Patrick did. In her view, Sister Richey became defensive and wouldn't listen whenever she voiced an opinion; which explained why she didn't make suggestions. She believed that Sister Richey was arrogant and had a holier-than-thou attitude. There was merit to these perceptions; but they were exaggerated and missed the important fact that her companion had many positive traits as well.

Her negative judgment of her companion changed some as Sister Richey made the changes described above; but unfortunately Sister Patrick remained basically focused on all that was not yet perfect about her companion, and failed to see the many positives. Sister Patrick also failed to see the problems in her own behavior-- clearly a mote and beam problem--which the Savior warned about in the Sermon on the Mount (Matthew 7:3). This made Sister Patrick a frustrated and unhappy missionary until she was finally transferred to another companion.

Avoid Judging Companions or Anyone Unrighteously

Although they probably didn't see it in this context, when they were emphasizing the other's faults, both Sister Richey and Sister Patrick were making an unrighteous judgment. They were not following the Savior's instruction to "Judge not according to your traditions, but judge righteous judgment" (JST John 7:24). Sister Richey and Sister Patrick had different personalities and they had grown up with different traditions. Much of what irritated them about each other boiled down to the fact that the other's behavior didn't match their expectation, or their own way of doing things. As is often true, in addition to focusing on their companion's faults rather than strengths; they were also assuming faults that weren't really faults at all, just differences in style and personality.

The truth is that our way of doing things may indeed be better, at least for us; and we generally don't have to change our traditions simply because others have different ones. On the other hand, we do need to avoid condemning others because of their different experiences and beliefs. It also helps to be open to the possibility that our traditional way of doing things is not necessarily the best or only way. Furthermore, when we join with those having different traditions in some common cause, like missionary service, compromise is usually required. Bull-headed insistence that others change to our way of thinking or doing things will never work.

Emphasize the Good in Ourselves as Well as in Others.

As suggested above, admitting our faults and taking responsibility to fix them is an important part of the repentance process. At the same time, it's also true that it does no good to demean ourselves or exaggerate our own faults as we attempt to overcome them. It's not hard to imagine the result if someone followed us around day and night constantly telling us how poorly we are doing, how we aren't trying hard enough, what a loser we are, and so forth. Yet, that's exactly what some missionaries do to themselves; likely with liberal help from Satan. Even though they may understand the doctrine correctly, those who do this fail to see who they really are.

Moses discovered who he really was, and who all of us are, when God appeared to him as described in the first chapter of Moses in the Pearl of Great Price. There Moses tells us that God introduced Himself as the Lord God Almighty, and reminded Moses that "there is no God beside me, and all things are present with me, for I know them all" (Moses 1:6). Moses was also shown the amazing breadth and scope of God's work (Moses 1:8). Further, Moses was affected physically by being in the presence of God. He fell to the earth when the interview ended, and it was several hours before his strength returned. (Moses 1:9-10).

On the surface, it might appear like this dramatic introduction was designed to impress Moses with how great God is. It's more likely that all of this was intended to set the stage for the earth-shaking revelation: "thou art my son" (Moses 1:4). God is indeed almighty, but we are His children. That makes Moses, and all of us, "heirs of God and joint-heirs with Christ" (Romans

8:17). As presumptuous, and even as blasphemous, as this may sound to some people, the scriptures reveal this to be fact. And nothing could be more significant than this truth in defining our eternal worth and potential.

Having an understanding of who Moses was from an eternal perspective greatly strengthened his confidence. A little later, now armed with this knowledge, Moses was able to confront Satan successfully with the perfect come back to temptation. When Satan wanted Moses to worship him, Moses responded by saying, "Who art thou? For behold, I am a son of God, in the similitude of his Only Begotten; and where is thy glory that I should worship thee?" (Moses 1:13). In theory, this understanding should also help any missionary when Satan comes tempting. It should also be good reason to never give up on ourselves. It is never correct for a child of God to think of himself or herself as a loser who has totally blown all chances for respect and honor. This truth has been taught by many prophets over time, including President Spencer W. Kimball:

> "You are unique. One of a kind, made of the eternal intelligence which gives you claim upon eternal life. Let there be no question in your mind about your value as an individual. The whole intent of the gospel plan is to provide an opportunity for each of you to reach your fullest potential, which is eternal progression and the possibility of godhood" ("Privileges and Responsibilities of Sisters", *Ensign*, November 1978, p. 105).

In spite of understanding all of this, Elder Bentley was one of those missionaries who had given up on himself. Elder Bentley was exposed to pornography at an early age and had been addicted for years. He was less than truthful during his worthiness interviews and was involved with pornography on and off right up until he entered the MTC. He had convinced himself that by serving a mission he would finally be able to put his longstanding habit behind him. And it did work out that way for a while. During the MTC and for a time after, he was sorely troubled with pornographic images and temptation; but he was able to distract his thinking and focus on his service.

As time went on, however, it became more difficult to say no to the images that kept coming to his mind. Masturbation again became a regular occurrence and he was even clever enough to find access to pornography while serving. He felt horrible about himself and soon came to the conclusion that all was lost. He believed that if he couldn't solve the problem on his mission, he never would. He constantly put himself down over this issue, concluding that he was a lost soul. In the process, he was making several mistakes in his thinking.

1. *He thought of himself as an evil person.* It would have been closer to the truth and a lot more motivating to see himself as a good person (in reality a child of God) who was involved in an evil activity. If he was an evil person, he wouldn't have felt so guilty about what he was doing. Rather than celebrating and accepting this behavior, he hated it; and he hated himself for letting it control him. Elder Bentley obviously had work to do; but as long as he hated the sin and desired to repent, there was hope.

2. *The fact that he had not yet solved the problem didn't mean that he never would.* Rather than focus on all of his failed

attempts, he would have been better off focusing on his accomplishments. In fact, he had been successful in overcoming his addiction over extended periods of time. It's always more motivating to focus on the times we are successful at something difficult than it is to focus on the times we fail. In this regard, sometimes we Latter-Day Saints are really "Ladder-Day Saints". We think of progress toward a goal as similar to climbing a ladder. When we slip and fall, it's as if we have fallen in a heap at the bottom of the ladder. We must then exert tremendous energy to just get back to where we were, let alone climb on from there. It's better to think of working toward a goal as being like balancing oneself while walking along a flat topped fence. It's not a particularly easy task, but generally possible. We may get distracted, get fatigued, or the wind may come up, causing us to lose our balance. At that point we need only to get back on the fence and keep going. Progress made toward the goal counts. We don't need to go back to the beginning and start all over again.

3. *Elder Bentley had assumed that serving a mission would make it so much easier to repent of the evil in his life; when in fact, it probably made it more difficult.* This is likely one of the reasons that honest and open discussion with priesthood leaders about worthiness is so important before serving. For a number of reasons, it's often easier to solve problems before rather than during missionary service. For instance, those addicted to pornography, or those who have similar addictions, will find that admitting the problem and seeking help from God and others is necessary to success. Wearing a name tag and representing the Savior can actually make that more difficult to do while serving. Working with groups such as the Addiction Recovery Program sponsored by LDS Family Services is also often an important

ingredient in recovery. Participating in such groups is generally not a possibility for serving missionaries. Furthermore, as mentioned in a previous chapter, frustrations are typically high and familiar coping mechanisms are generally unavailable to serving missionaries, all of which can make recovery more difficult. Finally, because of the damage they do to Satan's cause, missionaries sometimes are a special target of the adversary.

4. *Elder Bentley felt that in order to solve his problem, he had to make it a priority in his life.* Elder Bentley thought about his problem a lot and was hyper vigilant, constantly monitoring his thoughts for anything inappropriate. The truth is that he was thinking about his problem way too much. Whether he was caving in to temptation, or trying really hard not to, he was still involved in the problem. A better strategy was to focus on things outside of himself and his problems. He found that by engaging in the lives of others and making their needs his focus, he experienced fewer unwanted thoughts; and those he had were easier to manage. By far, the easiest times in avoiding temptation occurred when he was fully involved in his mission work and less focused on himself.

Obviously, Elder Bentley needed to bring this problem up to his Mission President, which he was finally able to do. With help from the Lord, which was much more powerful once he was honest with his priesthood leader; and help from his Mission President and a Mental Health Advisor, he was able to resolve the issue and stay on his mission. Even if he had not successfully resolved the problem; and/or if his priesthood leaders determined that his past and current behavior required that he be released from his mission, it would still not have been the end of all hope. As suggested above, there are resources at home, that when taken advantage of, would actually increase the chance of successfully overcoming his addiction. And in general, no matter the number of failures, there is always hope as long as we continue to try; especially if we do things the Lord's way, which Elder Bentley was finally able to do.

The Importance of Gratitude

During his effort to overcome his addiction, Elder Bentley also found that being grateful was a big help. This was true in part because gratitude naturally results in us focusing on the positive rather than the negative. Gratitude is a big part of having a positive and optimistic outlook in life. Also as pointed out by Elder Neal A. Maxwell, gratitude takes the focus away from our self; which is so much healthier than the overdone self-focus that at first held Elder Bentley back.

> "God experiences a deep, divine disappointment in us when we are ungrateful and when we are unwilling to confess God's hand in all things. (D&C 59:21). But it is because of what our sustained ingratitude does to us, not to Him. Failure to see His hand in human affairs in bringing to pass His eternal purposes and plans in the world (at the same time leaving us to exercise our agency) is a fatal misreading of life. It also represents a profound spur to selfishness and self-centeredness. It is these faults which lead to the celebration of the appetites rather than of spiritual things". (Neal A. Maxwell, *Sermons Not Spoken*, Deseret Book, 1985, p. 85).

Being grateful for God's blessings and for the help we receive from others naturally helps us avoid selfishness and self-centeredness; along with the inevitable darkening of our soul that occurs when we are self-centered. There are also a number of other benefits that accrue when we remember to be grateful. Three of these benefits that are particularly relevant to missionaries are as follows:

Expressions of gratitude are often more powerful than criticism. Sister Taupu had a problem with her disorganized and messy companion. She was always stumbling over her companion's clothes and other items that were typically strewn around in their general living area. She was also frequently upset when she had to work around her companion's personal items typically left in the bathroom. She had asked for cooperation any number of times; but so far to no avail.

One Sunday Sister Taupu found the bathroom to be even more of a disaster than normal. This was very frustrating and her anger continued as Sister Taupu and her companion hurried off to Church. All during the first part of their Sacrament meeting, Sister Taupu kept thinking of all the times she had put up with her companion's mess and how unfair it was. She thought of exactly what she would like to say to her companion at the first opportunity; none of which was at all complimentary. Then as she was preparing to partake of the Sacrament, the Spirit reminded her of an old adage that she had been overlooking: "You get far more with honey than you do with vinegar". After participating in the Sacrament she started to review all of the things that she appreciated about her companion. Immediately, she began to feel less anger and the Spirit began to help her see even more positive things about her companion. Soon she had a relatively long list of positives in mind.

Later that night, rather than give her companion the stern lecture she had originally planned, she reviewed with her companion the list of things for which she was grateful. The result was a wonderful feeling experienced by both Sisters Taupu and her companion. Their relationship was strengthened and they both went to bed with a good feeling that helped them rest soundly. The exact opposite result is likely if Sister Taupu had followed through with her original intent. Then by continuing to look for and be grateful for the good in her companion over time, two additional benefits became obvious to Sister Taupu. She found that her companion, without being lectured to, did a better job of cleaning up after herself. Apparently you do get more with honey than vinegar. Beyond that, the residual messiness just didn't seem to be such a big deal to Sister Taupu; all of which made her a more comfortable and happy missionary.

Gratitude will improve our daily mood. Anything we can do that will help us think about the good things in our life will likely make a positive difference. Missionaries can encourage gratitude by simply counting blessings, as recommend in a favorite hymn (Hymns, No. 241); or perhaps establishing a formal goal will help. For example, consider taking a minute or two as part of your bedtime routine to write down at least three good things that happened that day. Just recognizing and reviewing the good things that have happened, or the general things in your life for which you are grateful, will typically elevate mood and optimism in the moment. Also, there is something magical about actually putting your thoughts on paper. At least it provides a written record that can be reviewed over time for added benefit. Since we seem to naturally take the good things in our life for granted, or fail to see them because we are so focused on the negative, it sometimes takes a formal effort to recognize and acknowledge the many positive things in our lives.

This is especially true of general or repeated blessings. Most of us are grateful for some special or extraordinary gift, but may fail to appreciate those that come repeatedly. In fact, we can sometimes become so accustomed to a particular favor, that we might expect and demand it. How do we respond, for instance, if someone we are relating to, who is generally thoughtful, in one instance is not? Do we get upset and frustrated because what was expected didn't happen, or do we look past the exception and appreciate the general rule? The prophet Lehi in the Book of Mormon was able to do this when his very faithful and generally supportive companion had a problem in one instance with his visions (1 Nephi 5:2-3). Rather than attack her and express disappointment in her momentary lack of faith, Lehi was able to comfort her (1 Nephi 5:6). Faithful Latter-day Saints, especially missionaries, often experience special "tender mercies" from God and others; but so much of what happens is general and repeated. Those are the kinds of blessings that often require special attention to appreciate.

Prayers of thanks are yet another way to build gratitude into our lives. Some of our most meaningful prayers are those in which we don't ask for anything; but rather take the opportunity to express gratitude for the many things which bless our life. Personally, I also find that a little silent prayer, a simple non-verbal "Thank you, Father", after something good has happened, adds to the positive feeling associated with some success.

Again, whatever we do that gets us thinking about the good things in our life will tend to improve our mood and optimism. Anything that tends to focus on our needs and wants, and/or the problems and obstacles in our life, is likely to do just the opposite.

Gratitude will help us deal with adversity. Having a grateful heart is a significant help when facing adversity. It's not easy to have a perspective of gratitude when things aren't going well, such as when there are serious problems with a missionary's family at home, or when there are major disappointments in finding and teaching efforts. There is no question, however, about how much it helps when missionaries can be grateful even during these times. I'm not talking here about trying to see the personal benefit in adversity from a philosophical point of view. That is always a good thing to do; but often difficult when in the middle of something that is going desperately wrong. What I am talking about is simply focusing on the positives in our life at the moment.

As an example of this, Elder McDonald just heard that his father had lost his job and that the family was hurting financially. His dad had actually been unemployed for some time and his family had kept the news from Elder McDonald. The financial pressures and other factors had also put a huge strain on his parent's marriage; to the point that there was now the real possibility of divorce. All of this was understandably upsetting to Elder McDonald and there were some important issues here that would impact his life after his mission; and the lives of his loved ones at home. Along with all of the negatives, however, there was at the same time a very long list of positives. Just to mention a few, both parents were in good health; mother had a good job; the

Bishop was aware of the problem and helping with needed Church resources, the ward was able to continue funding Elder McDonald's mission, and so forth.

Elder McDonald could choose to focus on all of the very real problems in his family at the moment; or he could choose to focus on the many good things that were happening at the same time. That choice made, however, he couldn't choose how he felt. He couldn't just decide to feel at peace while continuing to focus on negatives. What he felt at any moment was an inevitable consequence of what he was thinking at the time. If he looked at his situation with gratitude, he felt happy and optimistic. If he focused on all that was wrong, he felt depressed and the situation looked hopeless. His faith in God's support, which he sorely needed, was also strengthened as he focused with gratitude on the blessings, rather than the challenges in his family's situation.

Think to Thank.

Along with having a grateful outlook and attitude, it's also important to express the gratitude we feel. One of the most famous lessons on gratitude in scripture was taught by the Savior with respect to the ten lepers who were healed (Luke 17:12-19). As you may remember, only one returned to give thanks. Being healed of leprosy was an amazing gift that, no doubt, all ten were equally thrilled to receive; but only one returned to express thanks to their benefactor. The others probably had the thought to do so, but rationalized the impression away, perhaps with thoughts like, "I'm too busy", or "It's too far", or my personal favorite, "He knows how I feel, and I don't need to say it." As indicated above, privately appreciating our blessings will be a blessing to us; but in order for gratitude to bless others; and in order for it to have its full impact in our lives, it needs to be expressed. Imagine the added blessing to the leper returning to express thanks when he was then able to interact personally with the Lord, and hear directly from the Savior, "thy faith hath made thee whole" (Luke 17:19).

With respect to publically expressing our gratitude, President Thomas S. Monson has suggested a useful motto that we would be wise to remember: "Think to thank". He suggests that "these three words are the finest capsule course for a happy marriage, a formula for enduring friendship, and a pattern for personal happiness" (*Pathways to Perfection*, Deseret Book, 1973, p. 254). He might have also added to the list, "thinking to thank" is critical to success as a missionary companion, success in working with local members, and success in finding and teaching investigators. When we "think to thank" we will return to express gratitude for our blessings from God; and we will find ways to communicate thanks to those around us who help us in some way. We will also find ourselves wanting to serve and do nice things for others. Gratitude is a basic virtue that naturally motivates us to be the best missionary, or whatever other good thing, we can be. With gratitude we do the right thing because we feel a desire to do it, not because we are compelled to do it.

In addition to its other benefits, gratitude, and the general habit of focusing on positive and not negative, will also help develop appreciation for God and His plan. These virtues will help missionaries see the Big Picture; that is, help them see the importance and scope of the grand cause in which they are engaged. Furthermore, gratitude, focusing on the positive, optimism, and being engaged in a noble cause are all important ingredients in resilience; which can be defined as the ability to bounce back from adversity. All of us, but especially missionaries, sorely need to be resilient in this life. This important ability is discussed further in the next chapter.

CHAPTER FIVE

MISTAKE FIVE: FAILING TO SEE THE BIG PICTURE

Missionaries are certainly taught, and they generally understand, the importance of the cause in which they serve. That understanding, however, can begin to buckle when faced with some of the frustrating details of their service. For instance, constant rejection can lead to conclusion that a missionary is wasting his or her time. Reluctant members, mission inefficiencies, unmotivated companions, avoidable mistakes, and a long list of other frustrations can all lead to the same conclusion. The obvious question then is how can missionaries remain optimistic, and have a sense of being engaged in a noble cause, when these kinds of obstacles are encountered?

Following is a discussion of five reasons why there is value and purpose in his or her service, even on a missionary's worst day ever. Seeing this purpose and value will go a long way toward helping a missionary bounce back the next day; and then keep going as additional frustrations are encountered.

There is Value and Purpose Even on a Missionary's Worst Day

There may be a positive outcome that can't be seen. Two missionaries serving in Germany were having a terrible day. Appointments had fallen through and they experienced nothing but rejection during their finding activities. As an example, one of those they approached on the street made it crystal clear that he had no interest in their message. Given his rude and abrupt response, the missionaries didn't push the point, but one of them did hand him a pass-along card and suggested that if he ever changed his mind he could look up information on the Church's web site. He angrily stuffed the card in his pocket and hurried off.

It so happened that this young man was generally not rude; and he felt guilty about his behavior, wishing that he had been less abrupt. When he was getting ready for bed, he noticed the card in his shirt pocket. The guilt he felt about his earlier behavior, and no doubt promptings from the Spirit, led him to access lds.org. The information he found there, and further promptings from the Spirit, led him to find a Church close to him and attend his first meeting. There the members and missionaries greeted him warmly; and he began taking missionary lessons, eventually getting baptized.

The problem for the missionaries who originally invited him to hear their message is that they will likely never know the rest of the story. This man had been visiting in the city where they met him; and he actually lived in a different town, which happened to be in the adjacent mission. He didn't have their names, and they didn't have his. There would be no natural way for them to connect with each other again. Here was an obvious case where missionaries had success that was not at all apparent at the time. The two original missionaries went home thinking that their day had been a total waste; but that was certainly not the case.

The Lord values effort and intent even when results are minimal. As taught in *Preach my Gospel,* "You are successful when you are obedient, live righteously, and do your best in helping others live the gospel." (PMG p. 11) Notice that there is no requirement here to also have a large number of progressing investigators and baptisms. The obvious reason for defining success this way has to do with the fact that obedience, living righteously, and doing one's best are all within a missionary's control. Given the agency of others, the number of baptisms and progressing investigators is not.

Unfortunately, this truth can be overlooked when establishing goals and reporting success in reaching those goals; which is an important part of a missionary's assignment. As President Thomas S. Monson has taught, "When performance is measured, performance improves. When performance is measured and reported, the rate of improvement accelerates" (June 2004, Worldwide Leadership Training Broadcast). For this and other good reasons, missionaries are asked to make weekly reports of the number of investigators baptized and confirmed, the number with a baptismal date, the number of lessons taught, and so forth. This information is often gathered and reported in Zone meetings and other public forums as well. Naturally, all committed missionaries want high numbers and their work will obviously be more fulfilling and exciting when they are teaching and baptizing regularly. It's also natural to recognize and congratulate those with high numbers; while those with low numbers are likely to feel a sense of failure.

This sense of failure can be motivating in some cases; but in others it can lead to feeling defeated. The response is more likely to be negative in situations in which, contrary to the instruction in *Preach my Gospel* (PMG p. 151), mission leaders overemphasize numbers, or even use control and manipulation, in an effort to increase them. For example, an Elder and his companion had experienced little success in their area. They dedicated themselves to extra prayer and effort and had a firm date set for the first baptism in the area in a long while. They were overjoyed; but when they called to share the good news in their weekly report, the response from their District Leader was, "Hey, that's great! But remember, the goal is to baptize four people in your area this month. Who else will be ready to go?" With this response from their leader, joy quickly turned to frustration and disappointment and it became apparent that, at least in the mind of the District Leader, it really was all about the numbers.

The goal then is to meld together the need to set goals and report on success in reaching those goals with the truth that real success lies in being obedient and trying to do ones' best. When honoring both concepts, missionaries will see the value in the goal setting and reporting process; and they will have a good attitude about it. When numbers are low, they will prayerfully seek answers regarding what they can do to improve the situation; and then be willing to work hard to make it happen. At the same time, they will realize the natural limits on the results of their efforts and judge themselves the way the Lord does. As Joseph Smith said, and as quoted earlier, "if you do your duty, it will be just as well with you as if all men embraced the gospel" (Joseph Smith, Letter to the Church, not after 18 December, 1933, Joseph Smith Papers, ID 1458). Doing ones' duty is what really counts, not blowing away "the competition" by having a high number of lessons and baptisms each week.

Being obedient and serving faithfully when results are meagre proves you are not a "fair weather" disciple. It's easy to be upbeat and feel great about yourself and the work you are doing when things are going well. It's not so easy to maintain a positive attitude and effort when there are no obvious results from the hard work. Knowing this, the Lord is likely to appreciate our diligence and commitment even more when we persevere through adversity. For one thing, our doing so is a statement of strong character. It shows us to be the kind of person that He can count on no matter what. That will certainly be one of the important conditions on our eventually receiving all of the blessings He has in mind for us (D&C 84:38). Our faithfulness through adversity is also a strong statement of love and support. When we do the right thing, even when there is no immediate reward for doing so, we are demonstrating love and appreciation for our Creator. That sounds like something well worth doing.

From an emotional/mental health standpoint, when missionaries hit a period when their best efforts don't seem to be producing that much, they will be better off thinking things like:

> This isn't much fun right now; but I want to prove myself to be someone that can be depended on, even when it's rough going.

> God knows I am working hard and trying my best. That should be good enough for me.

> I understand that mission leaders are concerned about the numbers, and so am I; but that isn't the most important thing.

I'm going to continue to push myself, be prayerful and work hard, no matter how long it takes.

It's darkest before the dawn. If I hang in, things are likely to improve.

I just need to think about what the Savior suffered for me (D&C 19:18; D&C 122). This is the least I can do for Him.

This last thought can be particularly powerful. Whenever we are feeling a little sorry for our self, it can be very helpful to review all that the Savior endured on our behalf. Our burden, however oppressive, will always pale in comparison.

It's important to the Lord that everyone has an opportunity to accept the gospel, whether they actually accept the invitation or not. In order for God to be the just God we know Him to be, at the end of the day, everyone must have an opportunity to hear the truth. That, of course, is part of the incentive behind the vast missionary effort taking place on the other side of the veil (D&C 138); as well as the great effort going forward here in mortality. It's also true that accepting the truth once heard is no simple matter. It usually takes preparation and multiple opportunities (invitations) before a person is ready to be baptized. Missionaries who get no further than presenting the name of the Church, hopefully in association with a friendly, smiling demeanor, have helped move the Lord's cause forward. There is benefit if an investigator gets no further than learning to pray, or having exposure to the scriptures. That's at least a start.

Given agency, and the requirements of faith, the missionary effort is inevitably inefficient. It seems like it would speed things along if there were many more dramatic miracles, such as Paul's conversion on the road to Damascus (Acts 9:1-12). It might help if God simultaneously co-opted every TV and radio in the world, sending a message to seek out the young men and women wearing name tags for an important message. God obviously has the power to do that and so much more; but that is apparently not the way He wants invitations to be made. In order for there to be no sense of coercion or force; and in order to maximize the requirement of faith and commitment, it must be the slow process of finding and teaching with which we are familiar. It's true that advances in technology can and will help "hasten the work" (D&C 88:73) in our day. For the reasons cited, however, it's still likely to be a relatively slow process requiring the combined efforts of all Latter-Day Saints.

With respect to the benefit of having more miracles in the work, before we get too excited about that possibility, we also have to consider the fact that miracles come after faith and are generally not that useful in building it (Mormon 9:19-20). Even when the Savior was on earth and ministered in great power, it was a slow process with minimal results. As Joseph F. Smith wrote, "I marveled, for I understood that the Savior spent about three years in his ministry among the Jews and those of the house of Israel, endeavoring to teach them the everlasting gospel and call them unto repentance; And yet, notwithstanding his mighty works, and miracles, and proclamation of the truth, in great power and authority, there were but few who hearkened to his voice, and rejoiced in his presence, and received salvation at his hands" (D&C 138:25-26). Maximum effort for minimal results seems to be the way it must be done.

Any great accomplishment requires great sacrifice. This is true in all pursuits of which I am aware. Great athletes certainly have talents in certain areas that most of us do not. Those talents, however, must be honed through hours of commitment and practice in order to produce consistently great performance. What is true of all worldly success must certainly be true when we are talking about accomplishments that will make a difference through eternity. To obtain those blessings, good coaching is required (as obtained from the Spirit and in scripture), as well as mistakes along the way, tests of faith, perseverance, and continued faithfulness in spite of all obstacles.

When things get really tough, we might well remember what Joseph Smith taught: "a religion that does not require the sacrifice of all things never has power sufficient to produce the faith necessary unto life and salvation" (*Lectures on Faith* [1985], 69). Which is perhaps part of the reason why the Law of Sacrifice has been such an important part of the gospel from the beginning (Moses 5:4-16). With regard to this law, we may not be asked to sacrifice a first born son as was Abraham (Genesis 22:1-18), or give our life as some early pioneers and others have done. Among other things, our sacrifice is perhaps more likely to involve patiently persevering in faith during times when it may appear that we aren't getting much from the effort.

It might also help when things get difficult to consider what the word sacrifice means. As we read in the Guide to the Scriptures found on the Church website (lds.org), "In ancient days, *sacrifice* meant to make something or someone holy". That may still be one of the best definitions. If missionaries realize that enduring disappointment could be a necessary part of the process of their becoming holy, it could give meaning to even one of their worst days. In modern times, the word sacrifice has now come to mean giving up or suffering the loss of worldly things for the Lord and his kingdom. This is obviously also an important and relevant definition. Missionaries experiencing disappointment and discouragement can count it as part of the sacrifice they are willing to make. Having this attitude should help them follow the Savior's direction, "Wherefore, be not weary in well-doing, for ye are laying the foundation of a great work" (**D&C 64:33**); or as Paul taught in Galatians, "And let us not be weary in well doing; for in due season we shall reap, if we faint not" (Galatians 6:9).

The forgoing five arguments can help missionaries see the value in even their worst day. Having this understanding will help them remember that they are indeed engaged in a transcendent work, even when on the surface it may not look like it. Having this realization will then help them be resilient in the face of the immediate disappointment they face; and it will also move them toward being more resilient in general.

This happened to a friend of mine who served a mission in France some years ago. His was a very difficult mission at the time. Most of his days were devoted to tracting and there were few opportunities to teach the gospel. At one point about four months into his service, he hit a crisis point. The constant rejection and routine got to him and he remembers feeling that he simply couldn't continue his mission. He couldn't face another day. He got on his knees that night and plead with the Lord for help--and nothing happened. He spent a restless night; but the next day he forced himself to get on his motor bike and he and his companion hit the streets once again.

It was at that point that an overwhelming and comforting feeling came over him; and quite unlike something he would normally do, he began to sing out loud "I Know That My Redeemer Lives" (Hymns, 136). In that moment my friend absolutely knew that he was not wasting his time. In that inspired moment, he wasn't promised an easy mission or future success in the work; but from that instant on, he knew that it would be worth it. In spite of the lack of obvious success, he knew that he was doing something the Lord valued and appreciated. This knowledge made all the difference and he was able to go forward and enjoy his mission. It's interesting to note, that this testimony did not come immediately after his pleading prayer. As is often the case, it came only after he made the decision to get up the next day and keep going.

What Is Resilience?

Resilience was earlier defined as the ability to bounce back from adversity. It's also a trait that allows us to endure adversity more effectively. Since the trait of resilience is one of the most important factors determining who will have a fulfilling mission and who will not; or for the matter, who will have a productive life and who will not, it's worth further discussion. The trait of resilience involves several factors as described below.

Resilient people don't ignore problems. They just let go of them quicker and shift attention to something positive. Two things suggested in earlier chapters can help missionaries do this. First, is yoking ourselves to Christ (Chapter Two) in a way that allows us not to worry about the things we can't control. Faith in the Savior, and in our relationship with Him, allows us to let go of negatives and turn them over to God; who is infinitely prepared to do what needs to be done about whatever the problem is. Second, when aware of negative thought about things that really don't matter in the long run; and/or things that we can't do anything about, we can follow the ADD strategy also mentioned in earlier chapters. This involves being aware (A) of unnecessary negative thinking, making a decision (D) that there is no value in dealing further with the problem; followed by distraction (D), which means changing the subject in our head to something positive. This simple procedure repeated over and over can be powerful in helping us become quicker to recognize and pull away from negatives; which in turn builds resilience.

Resilient people see challenges as an opportunity, not a threat. English is a second language for Elder Romero; and he had very little language training or public speaking opportunity before his mission. Soon after his arrival in the field, he was asked to give a talk in an English speaking Sacrament Meeting. Naturally he was stressed when he thought about this assignment. But imagine how stressed and insecure he would feel if he thought things like: "This is too hard. My English is not good enough. I don't know what I'm going to say. I'm going to make a fool out of myself." Conversely, he would be a lot less stressed and more confident if he thought things like: "This is a challenge, but it will be good for me. I know the Lord will help me. My English doesn't have to be perfect to convey the Spirit.

Since Satan's goal is to disrupt any righteous effort on our part, it's not surprising that Elder Romero was tempted to think in the more negative way. He also had to overcome a tendency to think generally in negative terms when facing challenges. To his credit, Elder Romero was able to recognize the temptation, whether coming from Satan or his own mind; and remember that he had a choice. Negative thoughts came me to his mind; but he exercised the power we all have to change them into something still truthful, but more positive. As with Elder Romero, bad habits can be broken, temptation overcome, and resilience developed.

Resilient people take decisive action to overcome their challenges. Elder Romero could fret and stew about how hard giving the talk would be and how it would likely result in disaster; or he could do what resilient people do and begin concrete steps toward preparing for the challenge. He could take out his planner and schedule time each day devoted to prayerfully considering what he might say in his talk. He could ask his companion for help. He could practice giving the talk. He could also put effort into thinking positively about the assignment. For example, whenever he noticed that he was worried about the talk, he could repeat a comforting scripture to himself such as, "Fear thou not; for I am with thee; be not dismayed; for I am thy God. I will strengthen thee; yea, I will help thee; yea, I will uphold thee with the right hand of my righteousness" (Isaiah 41:10)—followed by moving his attention to something else rather than dwelling on the issue.

There are actually a number of concrete steps Elder Romero could take in preparing to give his talk. But whatever he chose to do, the simple fact of actually doing something, as opposed to just worrying about it, is the critical factor. Motivation and confidence, as well as spiritual guidance, are often experienced once we are actually involved in a task, not before we begin.

Breaking a challenging task down into bite size chunks and moving forward step by step is always the best strategy; sometimes even ahead of having a clear vision regarding how to proceed or the confidence to do it. Resilient people tend not to hesitate too long; but they get started on projects and then fine tune their approach along the way.

Resilient people have caring and supportive relationships with others. This may be one of the most important characteristics of resilient people. Anything a missionary can do to promote close relationships with family, companions, other missionaries, investigators, and members will pay dividends. Holding grudges, putting up walls to close relationships, and distrusting others will all get in the way of developing resilience. Those missionaries for whom it doesn't come naturally should consider pushing themselves socially. Go out of your way to smile and be extra friendly in District and Zone meetings. Ask questions, participate in meetings. Be warm and open with investigators and members. True, missionaries who are clinically shy may need to go at this in a measured way; but it will still be necessary to set goals and to take concrete action. Blaming others, or concluding that this is just the way I am, will obviously not be helpful.

It can sometimes also help when going into a new area, or meeting people for the first time, to think something like: "These people don't know me. I can be anyone I want to be. I'm going to act like I am a confident, outgoing, caring person; whether I actually feel that way or not". It can further help to understand that one need not be the center of attention, or the life of the party, to be successful socially. Basically, all it takes is to genuinely care about others and to be interested in them. We all crave acceptance from others; and we all, even very shy people, have that gift to offer others.

In addition to close relationships with others, and perhaps most importantly, missionaries who have a close relationship with the Savior will be more resilient than those who do not. Probably the best formula for strengthening this relationship is obedience to the missionary rules and routine. Gospel study and service are the best ways available to improve our relationship with God. Those who do so develop real faith in the promise the prophet Alma gave to his son Shiblon, "As much as ye shall put your trust in God even so much ye shall be delivered out of your trials, and your troubles, and your afflictions" (Alma 38:5).

Resilient people keep things in perspective and consider even painful experiences in a broader context. Having a long-term perspective and seeing trials in a broader context is contrary to our "natural man" instincts. Even missionaries may be tempted to see things in a finite and limited way. On the other hand, resilient people see the pain as a means to a gain. They would agree with the Lord who said, "All these things shall give thee experience, and shall be for thy good. The Son of Man hath descended below them all…Therefore, hold on thy way…" (D&C 122:7-9).

Highly resilient people might even go so far as to welcome adversity. For example, "I'm glad my companion has the problems he does. This gives me a chance to develop more patience." "I wish we still had a car; but at least I'm going to be able to get back in shape by walking and biking." "I'm intimidated by the responsibility to be a Sister Training Leader; but I know it will help me develop the leadership qualities I lack." "I was so hoping for a transfer, but there must be a good reason why I will be staying here." "I hate the fact that she shared what I told her in confidence; but now I have a chance to practice forgiving."

Resilient missionaries will have no trouble understanding and believing the Lord who said, "He that is faithful in tribulation, the reward of the same is greater in the kingdom of heaven. Ye cannot behold with your natural eyes, for the present time, the design of our God concerning those things which shall come hereafter, and the glory which shall follow after much tribulation. For after much tribulation come the blessings" (D&C 58:2-4).

Resilient missionaries have confidence that, with the help of the Lord, they can influence and in many cases even control outcomes. Resilience goes together with confidence. It involves the belief that with imagination, effort, input from others, and input from the Spirit, we can generally make things turn out the way we want them to. This "can do" attitude is tempered with the understanding that some things are beyond our control and must be accepted. This combination of positive attitude and acceptance of reality allows the resilient person to concentrate energy on what can be accomplished rather than on what is beyond his control. It contrasts with thinking that we have no power in the world and are at the mercy of events.

As a practical example of this, two missionaries serving in a small ward with relatively few active members were asked by the ward bishop to organize an open house for the community. The Senior Companion, Elder A, is an optimistic and resilient missionary; while his companion, Elder B, is not. There were therefore predictable differences in how they thought about and approached the assignment. Elder A prayed with faith and began to brainstorm with his companion and others about how this activity could be carried out. He made a list of people to contact and things to do to make it happen, along with a timeline for developing and implementing a specific plan. His companion, on the other hand, didn't do anything other than make negative comments such as, "the ward is too small". "We can't get them to do the basics, let alone something like this." "I just don't think there is enough interest in the community. No one will come."

Elder A had his doubts as well; but he decided to operate on the assumption that how would they ever know unless they tried? He believed that there would be value in the effort no matter what; and he trusted that the local members would rise to the occasion. He therefore approached the local members with optimism and excitement. Elder A's excitement was catching and enough ward members became involved that a plan for the open house was developed and carried out as planned. However, the results were not as hoped. The activity was sparsely attended and the only non-members to come were those invited by the missionaries.

The disappointment confirmed Elder B's negative attitude, and he felt frustrated and down about the whole thing. Showing his resilience, Elder A took comfort in the fact that they had followed through with the Bishop's request to the best of their ability. He recognized that, even if results were not as hoped, the effort was a learning opportunity and it had a positive effect on many of those involved. It should be obvious which attitude is the healthiest and will contribute best to a successful mission and life.

Life is challenging and constantly changing and it takes an attitude like Elder A has developed to cope with it effectively.

Obstacles to Resilience

There are a number of factors that can block efforts to become more resilient. Two of the most significant obstacles that keep many missionaries from developing more resilience were identified in an *Ensign* article written by an LDS therapist who has had many years of experience working with missionaries (Lyle J. Burrup, "Raising Resilient Children", *Ensign*, Mar. 2013). In Brother Burrup's experience, which agrees with mine, the most common factor undermining resilience in new missionaries is a misunderstanding of the commandment to be perfect (Matthew 5:48). This important issue is discussed in the next chapter.

CHAPTER SIX

MISTAKE SIX: GOING OVERBOARD WITH GOOD THINGS

Sister Ariel had an experience on her mission that proved to be a classic example of going overboard with a good thing. Sister Ariel was a special missionary. She had a great spirit about her and a definite commitment to her missionary service. One day in a District Meeting, someone brought up the subject of a cleansing fast. By that, the Elder making the suggestion meant a process of identifying something of value that you would be willing to give up for a period of time in order to draw closer to the Spirit. Sister Ariel was a bit of a perfectionist and wanted to be the perfect missionary. The idea of a cleansing fast seemed like an excellent "extra-mile" activity; and she committed herself to do it. In terms of things she valued, she had a boyfriend serving in another mission and the emails she shared with him were a highlight of her week, as were the contacts she had with other friends and her family back home. Additionally, she loved music, which she would typically hum to herself all day long. This was not inappropriate music, just hymns and other music that she enjoyed.

Sister Ariel pledged that she would cease emailing her boyfriend, or anyone back home; and that she would even refuse to think about them for a forty-day period. She also vowed to avoid all music in her head for those same forty days. Of course, music and thoughts of her boyfriend and family did pop into her head; which she found continually frustrating, but she made a valiant effort to remove such thoughts whenever she noticed them. She was not long into this exercise when she began having intense headaches, nausea, and she was becoming quite fatigued. This progressed to the point that she was referred to a local physician who could find nothing wrong with her physically. Eventually the Area Mental Health Advisor was brought in for consultation. Two of the first questions he asked were how long she had been hurting; and if anything unusual had happened about the time her symptoms began.

There was a long silence on the line as it dawned on Sister Ariel that her physical problems all started soon after going on the cleansing fast. It became apparent that her physical problems were stress related, triggered by the unnecessary and extreme cleansing fast that she had undertaken. The fact that she generally put too much pressure on herself to be perfect was also a factor. Her health returned to normal when her missionary routine returned to normal; and when she made inroads into changing her long-standing habit of needing to do things perfectly.

Sister Ariel's experience is evidence of the wisdom in instruction offered by Elder Cecil O. Samuelson Jr. at the Provo Missionary Training Center, "Just as we should not lower the standards that the Lord has established for the conduct of His servants, we are also not authorized to raise them…Be sure that you do not have higher standards for yourself or others than the Lord has established" ("Perfection, Perceptions, Pressures, and Principles", Provo Missionary Training Center devotional, March 19, 2001, 2-3). No matter how well motivated, Sister Ariel's cleansing fast definitely exceeded normal missionary standards, as well as common sense. Her general problem with perfectionism also contradicted an important idea taught by Elder Russell M. Nelson when he said, "Men are that they might have joy—not guilt trips" (Russell M. Nelson, "Perfection Pending", *Ensign*, Nov, 1995, 86). Sister Ariel had her passport stamped with a very large number of guilt trips.

Additionally, Sister Ariel's problem illustrates the need for balance as missionaries approach their assignment. How does a missionary balance the need to give everything they have to their mission with the need to make sure that they don't run faster than they have strength (D&C 10:4)? In short, unnecessary guilt, perfectionism and not finding a proper balance were all a part of Sister Ariel's health crisis. Each of these subjects is discussed next in more detail.

Unnecessary Guilt

Once she accepted the challenge of her cleansing fast, Sister Ariel felt guilty whenever she thought of her boyfriend, or her family and friends back home. Likewise she felt bad whenever she noticed that she was again humming a tune to herself. Of course, there was no legitimate reason to feel guilty about any of this. If she had confessed what she was doing to her Mission President, he would likely have been concerned that she was feeling guilty about such things; and he would have tried to talk her out of being so extreme. He would likely have tried to build her confidence in the fact that she was doing a great job before the fast; and she needed only to continue her normal effort.

As another example of unnecessary guilt, an Elder felt guilty that he wasn't learning French as fast as he should. He kept comparing himself with his companion and others who had been on their mission longer, and/or who had a facility for languages. He kept thinking that he must not have enough faith, or he must not be trying hard enough. When he shared his problem with his Mission President, he was asked several questions. Are you praying sincerely for help? Are you following the recommended missionary study program? Are you trying to speak French as often as you can when out and about? The answer to each question was yes, which led the Mission President to conclude: "Well then, you have nothing to feel guilty about. Quit worrying and just keep doing your best. I'm convinced the Lord accepts your effort and He must not be concerned about your problems with French. If in the Lord's opinion, the problem was significant, He has the power to help you solve it."

As confirmed by the Mission President, guilt in this situation was unnecessary. Guilt was actually making it harder to learn French, and it was detracting from this Elder's enjoyment of his mission. The Mission President's advice was basically for this Elder to make sure he was doing his duty and then persevere. He should just keep doing what he could and not worry about the rest. This is essentially the advice found in the Doctrine and Covenants, "Therefore, dearly beloved brethren, let us cheerfully do all things *that lie in our power*; and then may we stand still (no worry, no guilt), with the utmost assurance, to see the salvation of God, and for is arm to be revealed" (D&C 123:17, italics and parenthesis added).

Contrary to the two examples just given, guilt is basically a good thing. Paul, and other prophets, have taught that guilt—which Paul calls Godly sorrow—"worketh repentance to salvation" (2 Corinthians 7:10). Guilt can be thought of as the moral equivalent of physical pain. If the body is functioning properly, putting a hand on a hot stove hurts. The pain is an effective warning that inevitable tissue damage will result if one's hand is not removed from the stove. Guilt, likewise, is a painful emotion that can signal the need to remove ourselves from conduct that will inevitably lead to emotional or spiritual damage.

Unnecessary guilt, however, has no redeeming quality and should always be avoided. Since it isn't always obvious, the trick is to determine whether the guilt we feel is actually unnecessary. The following questions might help when trying to sort this out:

1. Would whatever you feel guilty about disqualify you based on the worthiness questions in the temple recommend interview? Is it something that would make you unworthy to partake of the Sacrament; or jeopardize your Church membership in any way? If not, the guilt is likely to be unnecessary. Just fix the problem and move on. Don't worry or feel guilty about it.

2. Likewise, is it something that would seem silly to confess? Would your priesthood leader wonder why you are worried about such a thing?

3. What is the result of the guilt? Is it motivating you to do good things; or is it contributing to negative feelings and a loss of motivation to do what's right? Guilt, to be of value, must motivate one toward repentance, not toward depression and anxiety.

4. What do people you respect think about it? Is it something they agree is cause for repentance?

5. Is the guilt you are feeling the result of an innocent mistake that you didn't intend to make? Is it because of something that you basically couldn't control? In these cases, guilt is not necessary or helpful.
6. And of course, what does the Spirit tell you?

Missionaries are sometimes tempted to do things that are clearly inappropriate; and in these cases they should use the guilt they feel to help motivate them to repent. Far too many, however, feel guilty when there is no good reason. The resulting stress is counterproductive and no doubt makes Satan smile. As suggested earlier, Lucifer will take advantage of any opportunity to tempt a missionary to do too much of a good thing. He knows this will sometimes derail a missionary as quickly as when he or she does a truly bad thing. Not only that, but this is a tool he can use on even great missionaries like Sister Ariel, who have proven resistant to more overt temptation.

The Need for Balance

A missionary's life can be out of balance in the sense of doing either too little or too much of the good things they are expected to do; or it can be out of balance in a more general sense, as illustrated in the lives of two missionary companions, Sister Ernesto and Sister Fairfield. Sister Ernesto is very committed to being an exactly obedient missionary. She pushes herself and her companion to use every minute of their mission productively. She is very uncomfortable with "wasting time". Sister Ernesto can always be counted on to do her duty; and she has the respect of her Mission President and priesthood leaders. At the same time, she is quite judgmental and critical of others. She lacks patience, and she is generally so focused on being obedient and busy that her relationships with others suffer.

Although it would devastate her to see it this way, Sister Ernesto is at least, to some extent, following in the steps of the Pharisees, who were condemned by the Savior. "Woe unto you, scribes and Pharisees, hypocrites! For ye pay tithe of mint and anise and cummin, and have omitted the weightier matters of the law, judgment, mercy, and faith: these ought ye to have done, and not to leave the other undone. Ye blind guides, which strain at a gnat, and swallow a camel" (Matthew 23:23-24). Being obedient and duty bound, which Sister Ernesto does so well, is of value and needs to be continued. On the other hand, Sister Ernesto also needs to learn to balance those good qualities with charity, tolerance and patience.

Sister Fairchild, on the other hand, is very accepting of others. People enjoy her company and she is fun to be around. Unfortunately, she isn't always very good about doing her duty. She pushes the envelope on mission rules at every opportunity, and there are many important things in her mission responsibilities that she isn't getting done. Both sisters are falling short of their potential, and need to make a course correction. In each case, it's a matter of moderating their strength just enough so that time and energy can be devoted to the missing ingredient in their life. As described below, the scriptures have advice for both of these sisters; and by extension all of us, beginning with advice for Sister Ernesto.

What scripture suggests about priorities and pacing ourselves. Sister Ernesto, or anyone like her, could take a lesson from the New Testament story of Mary and Martha (Luke 10:38-42). Mary and Martha were sisters who invited the Savior into their home. Martha was very much into the mechanics of the event—food preparation, cleaning up and so forth—while Mary was involved directly with Jesus, socializing with him and "hearing his word". At one point Martha became upset that Mary wasn't helping more and asked the Savior to intervene. "Lord, dost thou not care that my sister hath left me to serve alone? Bid her therefore that she help me." To which Jesus responded, "Martha, Martha, thou art careful and troubled about many things. But one thing is needful and Mary hath chosen that good part, which shall not be taken away from her" (Luke 10:41-42).

The full story isn't presented in the account in Luke, but I like to think that it was a matter of priorities and timing. The necessary tasks associated with the event that so concerned Martha were important; just not that important, or important at the moment. In fact, I assume that Mary was willing to do what needed to be done, but not at the expense of something much more important at the moment. It's also likely that Martha valued her relationship with the Savior and His teachings, as well as her relationships with the others at the activity, and would have enjoyed being more social. She probably understood that the gospel message the Savior had for these sisters, and developing a relationship with Him, was more important than any temporal consideration. But her priority at the moment was being a good hostess, which made Mary's decision to sit and listen to the Savior look to Martha like wasting time and escaping responsibility. But Mary's choice was actually so much more than that. Developing a close relationship with another, and or connecting with the Spirit, often requires a certain amount of what may seem like wasting time.

As an example, a young couple seriously considering marriage will typically spend a lot of time talking—or just being together—without a particular objective, or any obvious product from their time together. An intimate relationship requires this kind of involvement. That same couple after marriage will sometimes become so duty bound, so busy, that they don't take sufficient time to just be together. Intimacy then suffers, as it always does when we spend too little informal and unstructured time with those, such as missionary companions, who we would like to get close to.

Perhaps the need for balance is also why the Lord was visiting socially with Mary and Martha in the first place; and why he attended weddings and other social events (John 2:1-10). In addition, He also took time away from duty and obligation to build his relationship with his Father. "And when he had sent the multitudes away, he went up into a mountain apart to pray; and when the evening was come, he was there alone" (Matthew 14:23).

The fact that multitudes were sent away means that there was more Jesus could have done if he had stayed at work. Taking time out to regroup and build his relationship with his Father came at the expense of those opportunities. But, of course, he made the right decision. He spent great effort and a lot of time on the multitudes and then backed away to spend some time regenerating, meditating, and reinforcing his relationship with his Father. Either of these activities without the other would have missed the needed balance.

This example of balance in the Savior's life is just one of many described in the scriptures; and the concept also comes up in the activities of God's prophets. Joseph Smith, for example, had many more important responsibilities than he had the time or energy to complete. During his work in translating the Book of Mormon, he was encouraged to be faithful in completing the task, to "be diligent unto the end"; but he was also advised to "not run faster or labor more than (he had) strength and means provided to enable (him) to translate" (D&C 10:3-4). This balance was a needed requirement in completing his assignment. King Benjamin in the Book of Mormon was known for his generosity in giving to the poor and administering relief to those who were suffering. He made clear in his teaching that this is an essential ingredient of a Christian life; but he also taught the need for balance in charitable work. "See that all these things are done in wisdom and order; for it is not requisite that a man should run faster than he has strength" (Mosiah 4:27).

As an additional example of the need for balance, the Lord gave Brigham Young some practical advice that greatly helped the early Saints in their forced exile from Illinois. Among other things, the Saints were given instructions regarding organization and provisions. They were advised to keep the commandments and to be prayerful. They were instructed to be diligent and wise stewards. But they were also advised to be merry and to sing and dance along the way (D&C 136:28). The need for balance from duty and obligation was important in spite of, or perhaps especially because of, the desperate circumstances involved in the Saint's exodus.

Of course, Sister Ernesto needs to continue to be an obedient missionary and to use her time wisely. At the same time, she needs to be less rigid about doing so; and she needs to find more time to ponder, meditate, relax, and build relationships with her companion and others—even though doing so may result in what looks like wasting time. Doing so is even likely to result in some important things not getting done. As an example, she would probably feel guilty about it; but it might be just the right thing after working hard at finding activities to sit on a park bench with her companion and just "hang out" for a few minutes before going back to work. If she isn't able to relax in this or other ways when appropriate, she is in danger of her many good works falling short of their goal. As the Apostle Paul suggested: "Though I bestow all my goods to feed the poor, and though I give my body to be burned, and have not charity, it profiteth me nothing" (1 Corinthians 13:3). Service motivated primarily by a sense of duty, or a life deficient in love and relationships, will be unfulfilling.

As for her part, Sister Fairchild also needs to change. She has charity and tolerance for others down well; and her social skills are commendable. She needs, however, to balance these assets by becoming more obedient and duty oriented. More will be said about what Sister Fairchild needs to do in Chapter Ten.

Strive for Perfection but Avoid Being a Perfectionist

It may appear that those committed to becoming perfect, like Sisters Ariel and Ernesto, are following a scriptural mandate. The Lord did say in the Sermon on the Mount, "Be ye therefore perfect, even as your Father which is in Heaven is perfect" (Matthew 5:48). Or, as modified by Joseph Smith to be even more directive, "Ye are therefore commanded to be perfect" (JST 5:50). Taking this scripture literally, it sounds like perfectionists are simply following a divine requirement. But does the Lord really expect us to do everything perfectly in this life, and become totally perfect in character? As part of the answer, I very much enjoy the story told by Robert Millet, former Professor of religion at Brigham Young University.

> "I remember the Sunday afternoon I turned to my wife and made a very serious commitment. We had been married but a few months and we were very happy. In a sincere moment I indicated that I had every intention of being perfect by the age of thirty. She smiled kindly and wished me well, and the matter was dropped. I really believed in what I was doing. I determined to read and study and pray and labor for the next several years, and then, after attaining the notable plateau, I would work to help others reach the same spiritual height.
>
> I suppose it isn't necessary to admit at this point that my goal was never quite achieved. Oh, I think I was a better man at thirty than I was at twenty-three, but I certainly wasn't perfect. Now almost twenty years after passing my initial goal, I still am not perfect in the sense I had originally intended to be, but I think I understand the process a little better now.
>
> I supposed, in my naiveté, if I just held my tongue, squelched my bitter feelings, blocked my thoughts, gritted my teeth, pushed myself to do my duty, and gripped the rod of iron white-knuckled-like for a sufficient time, that

eventually such things would become quite natural and second nature to me. And I admit that many of what were once quite labored actions are now a bit more spontaneous. Over the years, however, I came to know that perfection in this life is not only difficult but impossible, at least as we usually define perfection" (Millet, Robert L., *Within Reach,* Deseret Book, 1995).

The observation that perfection is impossible, at least as we normally define the term, goes along with the teaching of Elder Russell M. Nelson.

"We need not be dismayed if our earnest efforts toward perfection now seem so arduous and endless. Perfection is pending. It can come in full only after the Resurrection and only through the Lord. It awaits all who love him and keep his commandments" (Russell M. Nelson, *Perfection Pending*, Deseret Book, 1998).

It's also important to note that the word "perfect" as used in scripture might mean something different than being without flaw or blemish in character and performance. The Greek word translated as "perfect" in the King James Version of the Bible can also be translated as complete, finished, and fully developed. Earlier in the 5th chapter of Matthew, the Lord is talking about love. He points out that most of us love our friends, but God loves everyone, including his enemies. Then in verse 48, we are commanded to be like God in that respect. We need to be complete or whole by loving our enemies as well as our friends.

In essence, when He commands us to be perfect, God isn't necessarily talking about having a perfectly clean apartment, avoiding all mistakes in our interactions with others, or completing our assignments flawlessly. But rather, he seems to be talking about becoming one who loves completely; in the sense of loving even those who mistreat us. Given this possibility, the pressure some missionaries put on themselves to do everything they do perfectly may not only be misplaced; it might also get in the way of meeting the higher requirement to love their enemies. Some missionaries, for example, have an especially difficult time loving companions or others whose behavior interferes with their effort to be a perfect missionary. Ironically, this often results in impatience, a judgmental attitude, and irritability—that is, quite imperfect behavior.

Unfortunately, missionaries who recognize that they have the problem described here might find it difficult to dial back a bit. For one thing, these are generally really good missionaries who understand the importance of their service and naturally want to do it well. In this respect, they may be concerned that tempering their desire to be perfect will start them on a slippery slide in the opposite direction. Given their commitment to do things to the best of their ability, and the fact that making mistakes and underachieving are naturally not desirable, that worry is an unnecessary, but still common concern. A further problem is how often missionaries are reminded in missionary conferences, and at other times, of the need to be exactly obedient, and to serve with their whole heart, mind, and soul (D&C 4).

These reminders are important and represent an important truth; but not one that needs to be of concern to those who are already giving their best effort. Eating right and getting plenty of exercise is critical to good health; and all of us hear repeatedly that this is something we should do. Unlike the majority of us for whom the message certainly applies, those who are already eating healthy and exercising will also hear the message; but need not be concerned when they do. The same holds true for missionaries in mission conferences who are already serving to the best of their ability. Of course, because of their extreme expectation, perfectionists will have a hard time believing that they are serving adequately (because they know they could always in theory do more). However, by any reasonable measure, they are in fact giving their whole heart, mind and soul to their service already. Like everyone in this life, they are not completely free of ungodliness and they don't do much of what they do perfectly; but they are still amazing. Their Mission President, often the same one pushing the missionaries to be more obedient and hard-working, will have no quarrel with their level of effort. In fact, he will often go out of his way to suggest in one-on-one sessions that these particular missionaries lighten up.

How do we know when we are pushing too hard to be perfect? As just suggested, it may be hard for missionaries to realize that they are going overboard with good things; which suggests the need for a definition. We are being a perfectionist whenever we can't be at peace and feel good about ourselves or others unless something is done perfectly. Wanting to do things perfectly is fine. Striving to do things as perfectly as circumstances will allow is the mark of a successful person. For any number of reasons, *needing* to do things perfectly is not so good.

For one thing, given the fact that in missionary service, but also in life generally, there are many things that we simply don't have the ability to do perfectly, *needing* to do things perfectly will certainly be frustrating and demotivating. Then too, some of the things we actually can do perfectly take so much time and effort that it's not possible to do them perfectly without sacrificing more important things. We then run into the problem addressed by Elder Dallin H. Oaks when he warned about spending too much time on even good things, when doing so comes at the expense of things that are better. As Elder Oaks said, "We have to forego some good things in order to choose others that are better or best..." (Dallin H. Oaks, ("Good, Better, Best", *Ensign*, October, 2007).

For example, a missionary may spend so much time writing the perfect email to everyone on his list that other important things don't get done on Preparation Day. Even though there may be good reasons to do it perfectly, the better choice might be to not write everyone on the list; and to be less complete with what is written. Keeping a journal perfectly may interfere with getting to bed on time or enjoying a few minutes at the end of the day with a companion. Missing a day here and there, or shortening the entry, might be a more perfect option in this case. In other examples, so much time may be spent on planning their service perfectly that some missionaries spend too little time actually serving. Other missionaries may be so determined to follow a lesson outline perfectly that they are oblivious to whisperings from the Spirit to take a different direction.

Other examples of needing to do things perfectly include a missionary who can't get to sleep because not everything that should have been done that day has been done. Missionaries are pushing too hard when they feel guilty (as opposed to disappointed) for having a low number of progressing investigators, even though they have worked hard and are trying their best to make good things happen. A missionary is over-concerned about a good thing if he or she can't be comfortable when leaving the apartment late for reasons beyond their control; such as when one's companion takes too long to get ready.

So many other examples could be cited as well. For instance, some missionaries can't relax because they feel that they must confess sins again that have already been brought up with priesthood leaders. Even though they quickly try to get back on track, some feel guilty when their mind wanders, even briefly, in study sessions or when teaching lessons. Others feel guilty when inappropriate thoughts (temptation) pop into their heads; even though they consistently put such thoughts out of their mind and refuse to dwell on them.

In terms of a general rule, missionaries are trying too hard to be perfect whenever they feel guilty about anything they do imperfectly for reasons beyond their control; and/or when they push themselves to do something perfectly, at the expense of things that are more important.

Problems Likely When Missionaries Push too Hard to be Perfect

Some of the problems associated with pushing too hard to be perfect have already been identified. These include unnecessary guilt, frustration, and demotivation; along with the tendency to spend too much time and energy on good things at the expense of those that are better or best. As described below, these unwelcome consequences go along with more specific problems, such as compromised health.

Perfectionists are more likely to have health problems.
Sister Ariel, in the earlier example, found that pushing herself too
hard did strange and unwelcome things to her body. This occurred
primarily because of the chemical changes in her body resulting
from chronic high stress levels. Stress is a normal part of life and
it isn't all bad. It can heighten perception, increase motivation, and
add interest and excitement to our lives; until that is, it gets too
high for too long. That's when physical problems are likely, such
as those experienced by Sister Ariel. The chemicals released in
our bodies during high stress prepare us to take extraordinary
action; but when those chemicals remain in our systems at high
levels over time, headaches, gastro-intestinal problems, problems
with sleep and appetite, and many other physical health problems
are possible.

I have known missionaries who were unable to keep food
or liquids down to the point that they needed to be hospitalized for
dehydration and malnutrition. These problems continued until
they were returned home, where even without further physical or
mental health treatment, their symptoms magically disappeared.
One missionary had dramatic seizures that were frightening to her
and anyone around her. An MRI was ordered, and as luck would
have it, she had one of her seizures while undergoing the
procedure. Surprisingly, the MRI revealed absolutely normal brain
activity even while the seizure was occurring. In other words, here
was proof that the dramatic physical manifestation was
psychosomatic, or stress induced. Vision problems, pain in the
limbs, chest pain as severe as any caused by a heart attack, and
other significant physical problems can all be stress related.
Additionally, chronic stress will often compromise the auto-

immune system, resulting in more colds, infections, and similar problems than normal.

Along with problems with our physical health, perfectionism, of course, also contributes to poor emotional and mental health. Those who need to be perfect in what they do tend to be unusually self-critical, which leads to lowered self-confidence; and can contribute to a sense of hopelessness—an important element in clinical depression. Since so much of what they expect doesn't happen, a perfectionist is likely to be pessimistic, even though they know better. As discussed earlier, pessimism contributes to poor emotional health in a number of ways. Given the likelihood that things won't work out perfectly, at least in terms of how a perfectionist defines it, anxiety and panic disorders are also more likely.

Perfectionists are likely to be irritable, intolerant, and have difficulty in interpersonal relationships. In addition to the negative impact on physical and mental health, perfectionists often have a hard time being tolerant and charitable in their thinking and actions. For instance, someone who is obsessed with proper nutrition, exercise, and/or physical appearance is likely to be critical of a companion who cares less about such things. A missionary who is a perfectionist about keeping mission rules will be particularly frustrated when partnered with a companion who isn't perfectly obedient and doesn't care enough about the rules. A meticulous missionary will find a messy companion to be extremely frustrating.

When these kinds of situations arise, a perfectionist is inevitably frustrated, which leads to unusual levels of irritability.

Their frustration is also very hard to hide from the companion who is so disappointing. They may be able to bite their tongue for a time; but criticism will still be obvious in their nonverbal behavior. It's also true that biting one's tongue is painful and doesn't usually last very long. Sooner or later the pressure builds and they feel compelled to say something. When that happens, the relationship with their companion is likely to be damaged and arguments ensue that can be highly stressful. However, holding frustration in is also highly stressful.

The only way to truly avoid a problem in this respect is to change one's thinking so that the whole issue loses much of its importance. If missionaries can decide that their companion matters; but their companion's frustrating attitude and behavior does not, they are emotionally home free. The attitude and behavior of their companion may matter to God and it may be flat out wrong; but they need not let it affect them emotionally in any significant way. When missionaries think this way, there is no need to make critical comments; nor is there pressure from holding in frustration. The whole issue no longer matters.

Of course this doesn't mean that suffering in silence or completely compromising one's values is the best solution in these situations. There are many things that can be done to improve the situation before deciding this is just the way it is. Ideas on steps to resolve these kinds of problems are discussed in other chapters. It should also be remembered that if a missionary is violating a significant mission rule, such as leaving the flat alone; his or her companion is obligated to report the problem to mission leaders.

Perfectionists tend to procrastinate; and they have trouble making choices and prioritizing. We are likely to procrastinate whenever our actions need to be perfect. In that case, we will tend to wait so long for the right conditions to arise and/or to develop the perfect response, that we lose the opportunity to do anything at all. For instance, suppose missionaries have an investigator in the hospital and the perfect response would be to visit and offer a blessing. Maybe transportation and scheduling conflicts make that difficult. Hopefully the missionaries involved won't wait until they can do it perfectly to do at least something. They may be able to call the investigator and express their concern; and/or they could call the Bishop or others who might be able to help right away. Missionaries who need to do things perfectly may not value such imperfect options; and they may feel pressure to wait until the perfect response is possible. But something is better than nothing; and nothing is exactly what will happen if they wait too long.

Needing the things we do to be perfect also means that we might wait until we are certain that our decision is exactly right before proceeding. I know a Sister missionary at the end of her mission who had been accepted at two universities. In order to attend the first semester after her return home, she needed to accept one of the offers prior to her release. Since there were pros and cons and a lot of "what ifs" associated with either choice, she simply couldn't make up her mind. The stress and anxiety she experienced over the issue was quite distracting to her missionary service; and it added a sour note to the end of her mission. Missionaries who need to know for sure that what they intend to do is 100% perfectly correct before proceeding, will have a very hard time deciding which investigators or members to visit; or what lessons to teach. Deciding what topic to speak on and preparing remarks for talks in Church can be agonizing. In fact, any decision, even a simple one, is difficult or impossible when what we decide has to be exactly right.

Additionally, the need to choose between good, better and best described by Elder Oaks, referenced earlier, becomes a real challenge for someone who needs to be perfect. How can one prioritize between options when everything is an "A" priority?

Perfectionists tend to confuse perfection with worthiness, which can have negative spiritual consequences. Quoting Elder Cecil O. Samuelson, "Occasionally, for well-motivated and highly devoted Latter-day Saints, confusion occurs about the differences between worthiness and perfection. Worthiness and perfection don't mean the same thing at all! We can be worthy while still needing to improve" (Cecil O. Samuelson, "What Does it Mean to be Perfect", *New Era*, January 2006). It's sad and a bit frustrating when a Mission President hears one of his best missionaries tearfully reveal how unworthy and unsuccessful he or she feels. He knows that such missionaries will have a hard time staying motivated; and that enjoyment of their mission will suffer. It's unfortunate when they miss the confidence and peace of mind that they actually deserve.

Unless they come to see the truth, some with this problem will simply endure and persevere, but under an unnecessarily heavy burden. Others will develop health problems to the point that they will need to go home for treatment. And still others will decide to quit trying. They then just float along and bide their time until release. In all cases, feeling that one must be perfect to be worthy of the Lord's blessings will have a negative impact. It's too hard to keep beating one's head against the wall trying to do the impossible. Something is bound to give. And sometimes that something is one's testimony. Some end up thinking something like "living the gospel is supposed to make me happy; but I'm miserable." They then blame the Church rather than recognize that the problem lies in their misinterpretation of the gospel's demands. Others drop out of activity in the Church due to the discomfort of forever falling short of expectations. Of course, dropping out of activity for whatever reason is likely to have spiritually fatal consequences.

Antidotes to Trying too Hard to be Perfect

The preceding discussion has hopefully made the case that missionaries are making a significant mistake when they push themselves too hard to do everything perfectly. Following are several suggestions on how to overcome this bad habit.

Think in terms of wanting to do things, not having to do them. "Have to" implies no choice. If I *have to* be out the door on time, that's it. If something comes up that makes me late, I will experience frustration or even panic, depending on the importance of what's going on. If I *want to* get out of the door on time, and have done everything within my power to make it happen; I can be OK even if I'm late. As suggested in Chapter Three, it makes good sense to get in the habit of describing everything we do as something we want to do, not something we have to do. After all, everything is a choice.

Turn worry about things you can't control over to God. This was also discussed earlier in Chapter Two. We don't have to do everything perfectly, just the best we can under the circumstance. Then we leave whatever problems remain in the hands of our Perfect Partner.

Use the magic words, "it doesn't matter". If you are upset about something, you might want to ask yourself, will I care about this ten years from now? Often what upsets us at any given moment won't matter even ten days from now. If missionaries remain faithful, it's very unlikely that the innocent mistakes they make, the imperfections they see in others, or any of the things they now do imperfectly will matter at all at the end of the day. Unless that is, they get so concerned about such imperfections that they fail to repent of the really important things; and/or lose hope and give up at some point.

Pray for help. This goes without saying. We are not in this alone. What we can't do on our own often becomes possible with the help of the Lord. Problems that can't be fixed are much easier to deal with when we are comforted by the Spirit.

Use the ADD strategy. This technique is generally useful and has been suggested earlier. The steps in this case are, (A) recognize that you are feeling compelled to go overboard on a good thing; or when you get frustrated because something doesn't turn out perfectly in spite of your good effort; (B) decide not to worry about it; and (C) distract yourself by getting off the subject and on to something else in your mind. Repeat these steps over and over as long as necessary until the unease, guilt, or pressure to do something perfectly goes away.

Don't Go Overboard Trying Not to Go Overboard. Missionaries who understand the problems associated with pushing themselves too hard are naturally motivated to break the bad habit.

Sometimes, however, they approach the effort with the same perfectionism that they are trying to move away from. When this happens, rather than find relief, they end up with just one more thing to feel bad about. Now they feel guilty about everything that they aren't doing perfectly; plus they feel guilty for feeling guilty about it! The antidote to this possibility lies in treating oneself according to priesthood principles as described in the next chapter.

CHAPTER SEVEN

MISTRAKE SEVEN: FAILING TO FOLLOW PRIESTHOOD LEADERSHIP PRINCIPLES

Sister Donald was convinced that she was failing as a missionary; and in fact, she hadn't been giving her mission her best effort lately. When she shared her concerns with her Mission President, he asked her to imagine that instead of interviewing with him that day, she had an interview with the Savior himself. She was then asked to imagine how that interview would go. As she walked into the room, how would the Savior react toward her? Would he have a scowl on his face and show displeasure in Sister Donald? Would the gist of the interview amount to the Lord complaining about her lack of effort? Or would he embrace her and thank her for her service. Would he be encouraging and understanding; or would he be condemning?

Even though she knew she probably deserved it, Sister Donald had a hard time imagining a scowling Lord lecturing her about her failings. She also knew that if that were the case, she would leave the interview discouraged and would probably give up altogether. Whereas, if she felt love and support, she would leave the interview highly motivated to get back on track in her service. And that is very likely what would have happened had the Lord actually conducted the interview personally. The Lord would know her willing heart and that she was keenly aware of her shortcomings. He would certainly understand that dwelling on the negatives in her case would simply discourage her; while focusing on her positives, showing love, and giving her a vision of the blessings still within her reach, would do just the opposite. The basic message would be, "I know you want to do a better job. I love you, I trust you, and I will help you"; not "You are a disappointment to me and you have to shape up."

The Mission President then proceeded to do what he imagined the Savior would do if he were, in fact, conducting the interview. He honestly complimented Sister Donald for the many good things she had been doing and for the fact that she realized that she could do more. He then spent some time making sure that Sister Donald had a plan for improving her effort and that she knew that he and the Lord loved her and trusted her; and that they would both help in any way possible. Her Mission President also made the important suggestion that Sister Donald treat herself more the way the Savior would. She had been so critical of herself and so negative in her thinking that her confidence had suffered; which explained in large part why her performance had fallen off. As a result of the Mission President following the Lord's management style, Sister Donald left the interview with renewed energy and commitment, as well as a plan for self-improvement.

The Lord's System for Managing Self and Others

Section 121 of the Doctrine and Covenants is a great place to look when trying to understand the principles of leadership taught by the Lord and followed by Sister Donald's Mission President. In Section 121 we are warned that it is part of our "natural man" tendency to abuse power.

"We have learned by sad experience that it is the nature and disposition of almost all men, as soon as they get a little

141

authority, as they suppose, they will immediately begin to exercise unrighteous dominion" (V. 39).

Even mission leaders, especially those who are young and inexperienced, may fall prey to this natural tendency. Of course, whenever power is abused, or under whatever circumstance, it contradicts how things are to be done under priesthood authority.

"That the rights of the priesthood are inseparably connected with the powers of heaven, and that the powers of heaven cannot be controlled nor handled only upon the principles of righteousness.

That they be conferred upon us, it is true; but when we undertake to cover our sins, or to gratify our pride, our vain ambition, or to exercise control or dominion or compulsion upon the souls of the children of men, in any degree of unrighteousness, behold the heavens withdraw themselves, the Spirit of the Lord is grieved; and when it is withdrawn, Amen to the priesthood or the authority of that man" (vs. 36-37).

Those who have been victims of the abuse of authority can take comfort in the fact that this is not how things are managed in heaven. The instruction in Section 121 goes on as follows:

"No power or influence can or ought to be maintained by virtue of the priesthood only by persuasion, by long-suffering, by gentleness and meekness, and by love unfeigned;

By kindness, and pure knowledge, which shall greatly enlarge the soul without hypocrisy, and without guile—

Reproving betimes with sharpness, when moved upon by the Holy Ghost; and then showing forth afterwards an increase of love toward him whom thou hast reproved, lest he esteem thee to be his enemy;

That he may know that thy faithfulness is stronger than the cords of death" (vs. 41-44)

The word "betimes" in the quoted scripture is not commonly used today, but means early, or quickly. The word "sharpness" in the scripture likely means clear and direct; not piercing or cutting. Putting this all together, any criticism should be communicated in a focused, clear and direct manner. And the criticism should come quickly; i.e., the criticism should be closely associated in time with the behavior being criticized; and it should be quick in the sense of brief. Long lectures are not recommended. Then most importantly, any criticism should be conveyed in a spirit of love and hope.

A Practical Example

Two Zone Leaders were very familiar with Section 121 of the Doctrine and Covenants; but unfortunately they weren't very good at applying the concepts taught there. The Zone Leaders were concerned about four Elders in their Zone who had a reputation for breaking mission rules. Local members complained about the lack of commitment on the part of these four Elders; and, although they were not guilty of serious sin, it was obvious that they were not serving as they should. The four Elders lived in the same flat and one day the Zone Leaders sat them down as a group and basically tore into them. Voices were raised, fingers were pointed, and comments were made such as, "None of you deserve to wear the name tag of a missionary. You are a disgrace to the Church and if you can't get with the program, you should go home." The lecture was one-sided, long winded, and heavy on anger. Whether intended or not, the focus was on shaming these Elders into becoming obedient and getting back on track in their service.

Not surprisingly, the Zone Leader's intervention did little good. Three of the Elders left the lecture angry at the Zone Leaders who they unfairly thought of as "holier-than-thou" hypocrites. They focused on what they perceived to be their Zone Leader's faults; rather than recognizing or admitting the obvious problems in their own behavior. If anything, these three Elders were less committed and more disrespectful after the lecture. The fourth Elder was relatively new to his mission. He was offended by the behavior of the other three Elders in the flat and wanted to act differently; but he lacked the courage to stand up to the other three and usually went along with their program. He left the lecture feeling misunderstood and hopeless about ever being the kind of missionary he aspired to be.

Relative to the management approach recommended in the scripture quoted above, the Zone Leaders attacked these Elders rather than trying to persuade them. They were impatient rather than long-suffering; abrupt and angry rather than gentle and kind; and there was little love shown, feigned or otherwise. Their approach was unkind and not based in pure knowledge. For example, they totally missed the fact that the situation and needs of

144

the fourth Elder were so different from the other three. The Zone Leaders were doing what they preached; and in that sense, were not hypocrites. They were, however, manipulative and calculating rather than approaching the Elders without guile. Then at the end, they left with no attempt to restore positive feelings—to show forth afterwards an increase of love. Certainly all four Elders now saw their Zone Leaders as an enemy.

There may have been nothing the Zone Leaders could have done that would have led these four Elders to repent. The odds, however, would have been so much greater if they had better followed the Lord's way of leading. This recommended management style is clearly defined in the verses quoted from the Doctrine and Covenants above; and it was illustrated in different aspects of the Lord's ministry.

Following are some of the characteristics of the Lord's leadership style, along with how the two Zone Leaders might have modified their approach in order to better follow Christ's example.

In priesthood leadership, the leader acts as a servant, not a dictator to those led. After the Passover meal, just prior to the end of His mission in the flesh, the Savior took the apostles aside and washed each of their feet. In doing so, the Lord demonstrated respect for his followers and a willingness to serve them. Jesus acknowledged his position before the apostles, "Ye call me Master and Lord: and ye say well; for so I am"; but then he taught the important principle that the leader should have an attitude of service toward those he leads. "If I then, your Lord and Master, have washed your feet; ye also ought to wash one another's feet.

For I have given you an example, that ye should do as I have done to you" (John 13:13-15). The Zone Leaders in the previous example were dictatorial in their approach. There was no sense of their being a servant of the Elders they confronted. Humility was missing; as were specific suggestions regarding what could be done to improve the situation; along with sincere offers to help.

A better approach would have begun by taking the four Elders aside individually and getting their take on the situation. If these Elders denied or minimized the problem, the Zone Leaders would need to be clear and direct regarding what they understood the problems to be. However, this could be done in the spirit of wanting to help, rather than simply condemning the Elders. It was possible to be respectful without minimizing the seriousness of the issues being addressed. Heartfelt testimony regarding the importance of the work these missionaries were all called to do would have been more helpful than demeaning and shaming these Elders.

In priesthood leadership, there is no force or compulsion. The apostles surrounding the table as the Savior washed their feet had all accepted invitations to join the Savior in His work. At least in the case of Peter and Andrew, it was a simple "come follow me" invitation; which was met with immediate acceptance (Matthew 4:19-20). There were no threats and there was no force or coercion to accept the Lord's invitation. As a result, they wanted to emulate his behavior and leadership.

This is how it has been from the beginning, both in priesthood service and in our lives generally. As he did with Adam and Eve on day one, God makes clear the inevitable consequence of our choices; but then leaves us to decide: "nevertheless, thou mayest choose for thyself" (Moses 3:17). Unlike some religious extremists in the world today; we are not threatened with beheading if we fail to comply with God's wishes. In fact, just the opposite. "...for he maketh his sun to rise on the evil and on the good, and sendeth rain on the just and on the unjust" (Matthew 5:45). Choice and agency are the hallmarks of the Lord's plan, not force and coercion.

Of course, the Zone Leaders didn't threaten death or injury if the Elders continued their disobedience. Waterboarding was also out. Still, their forceful, coercive message contradicted the spirit of the Lord's example; and it created resistance to hearing the important message that the Zone Leaders were trying to convey. True, the Zone Leaders were correct in observing that the disobedient behavior was unacceptable in missionary service. But these Elders still needed to be respected and their choice acknowledged. The Zone Leaders might simply have identified the problem and then borne testimony of the value in obedience and the importance of the work all missionaries are involved in; followed by expressions of love toward the Elders being addressed.

In priesthood leadership, the focus is on the one. It's worth noting that the ordinance of washing the apostle's feet was performed for each apostle individually. Even though less efficient, this emphasis on the individual fits the pattern the Lord had earlier taught his disciples. "How think ye? If a man have an hundred sheep, and one of them be gone astray, doth he not leave the ninety and nine, and goeth into the mountains, and seeketh that which is gone astray?" (Matthew 18:12).

147

In our assignment as Area Mental Health Advisors, my wife and I saw any number of examples of this principle in action. For instance, on one occasion we were asked by the Area Presidency to travel with a Mission President to a remote island in the Pacific to meet with a missionary who had been sent home early from his mission for sending his companion to the hospital in a fit of anger. The trip was costly in time and money, but was needed in order to provide anger management training not available locally. Providing this information, and offering encouragement to this young man, was a wonderful and very spiritual experience for us. It clearly demonstrated how much the Lord cares for each of his children, even those who have made serious mistakes.

With this principle in mind, and referring back to the Zone Leader example, a confrontational interview would have been held only after being led to do so by the Spirit; and after considerable time working with each Elder individually in order to get to know him. Then if a formal interview was called for, it would have been conducted in private with each Elder separately. This would have been logistically more difficult and it would have taken more time. However, the effort could then have been better tailored to the individual missionary and it would have been easier to maintain a relationship of friendship and trust. This would have been especially helpful to the fourth Elder, who really did want to be an obedient and effective missionary. He, in particular, was truly a lost sheep who needed understanding, love and support; not threat and brow beating. Actually, each of these four Elders needed to hear from true shepherds whose voice they could recognize and trust (Alma 5:59-60); not sheep herders who were trying to force them in the right direction through intimidation and fear.

Additional Examples of Exercising Priesthood Principles in Leadership

Not surprisingly, the priesthood leadership principles discussed above are incorporated in the Preach my Gospel manual; which along with the scriptures, is the core instrument in training missionaries. Specifically as taught in Preach my Gospel (PMG, p. 151), mission leaders are asked to show interest in the lives of those they lead, which practically boils down to spending time with them and getting to know them. They are taught to look for opportunities to honestly praise those they lead, and recognize accomplishments toward reaching goals; remembering that positive reinforcement is more helpful than criticism, threat, or punishment in encouraging long-term progress. Leaders are asked to look for areas where there are training needs, and then to demonstrate specific examples of what needs to be done. It is also suggested that mission leaders show interest in the lives of those being taught, not simply in the numbers; and that there be no control or manipulation in their leadership efforts.

This last point about focusing on people and not numbers; as well as avoiding controlling and manipulative leadership practices, sometimes becomes an issue when setting and reporting on missionary goals. As suggested in Chapter Two, setting and reporting on goals is an important part of helping missionaries achieve their full potential. Unfortunately, however, it is also an area in which many missionaries feel an unhealthy pressure. Again from Preach my Gospel, the following are guidelines regarding goal setting that can help avoid this potential problem.

1. A goal is reasonable if it is specific and realistic (PMG p. 146). Vague goals such as "have more faith", "work harder" and "be more obedient" are not that helpful. On the other hand, specific and measurable goals designed to reach the objective of having more faith, working harder and being more obedient can be effective. Examples might be a goal to contact more people than normal each day during a short reporting period (the specific number depending on local conditions and recent experience); or a goal to memorize and study specific scriptures over some period of time. In terms of being realistic, goals that most missionaries will not attain, in spite of their best efforts, are somewhat common in missionary work; but clearly not realistic.

2. Missionaries should evaluate the effort they have put into achieving their goals on an individual basis; and then either seek a better approach/more effort where possible; or when that isn't practical, adjust the goal to better meet their ability and circumstance. (PMG 146) Not all missionary areas are created equal; nor do all missionaries have the same experience and ability. Goals should be adjusted accordingly.

3. Goals should include steps in the process leading to an overall desired objective; not just the overall objective itself. In other words, sub-goals are important, which

define steps along the way; and which can be measured on a daily and weekly basis (PMG 146).

4. Goals should not be thought of as quotas imposed on missionaries and their companions. In other words, goals should not be presented with the clear implication that anyone who doesn't reach the goal has failed as a missionary (PMG 146).

5. With respect to the goal setting process, it's helpful to avoid any suggestion that the goal is more important than the people involved. As it says in Preach My Gospel, "You are successful when you are obedient, live righteously, and do your best in helping others live the gospel" (PMG p. 11. Also, "The ultimate measure of success is not in achieving goals alone, but in the service you render and the progress of others" (PMG p. 146).

Perhaps an explanation for why this approach to goal setting, as well as the principles of priesthood leadership in general, are so important can be found in a performance model first advanced in organizational psychology years ago (Mason Haire, *Psychology in Management*, New York: McGraw-Hill, 1964, pp. 162-180).

The Quasi Stationary Equilibrium Model

This model suggests that performance is always in a state of flux and goes either up or down depending on the strength of various forces affecting it. In the case of Sister Donald, and other missionaries in general, this model can be illustrated as follows:

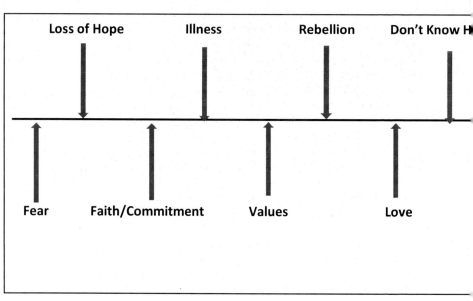

The horizontal line represents the level of a missionary's performance.

There are a number of forces that, when present, will lower performance. For instance, as shown in the above illustration, when a missionary is discouraged, sick, angry, or lacks knowledge about how to do his duty, performance will naturally go down. Of course these factors are just several among many. Disobedience, succumbing to temptation, companion struggles, and problems with mission leaders, pride, and any number of other factors will also depress performance. On the other hand, there are a number of factors that will naturally elevate performance. Among these, and included in the above illustration, are the faith and commitment of the missionary which compel him or her to do a good job. The values a missionary has, such as being dependable, working hard, serving others, humility, and so forth; will also naturally improve performance. Then there is perhaps the greatest natural motivator of them all--love. We know this was the primary motive behind God's willingness to make the supreme sacrifice in our behalf (John 3:16). Missionaries who love the Lord and the truth will naturally be motivated to serve with everything they have.

Fear is also shown in the illustration as a force that will increase performance. Indeed, a missionary may work harder out of the fear of displeasing God, mission leaders, or family and friends. The problem with this force as a motivator, however, is that it can also work to suppress performance. Fear of making a mistake, fear of disappointing others, and other kinds of fear will all hold a missionary back. It's also true that fear can at some point contribute to rebellion and disobedience; or other factors that hold back performance. In other words, any negative pressure that is pushing a missionary to do better may also increase some of the negatives on the top of the line in the above illustration; which will then eventually depress performance.

This suggests that if missionaries or their leaders want to improve performance, punishment and fear are not the best motivators. They might instead focus on increasing the positive factors that naturally increase motivation, such as faith and love. Missionaries generally understand that the best way to build faith, commitment, and love; while also instilling and maintaining good values, is by basic gospel study, prayer, and service—things missionaries are already doing if they are obedient. Investing fully in their missionary service and obediently following the guidelines for gospel study and service outlined in Preach my Gospel will increase both motivation and ability to serve effectively; and that will happen as a natural consequence of their effort.

The other option, and probably the most useful one in improving performance, is to reduce inhibiting factors that are on the top of the linc in the illustration above. When this happens, performance will naturally rise because of the forces on the bottom of the line. In essence, when factors suppressing performance are eliminated or reduced, performance will float up naturally and will not have to be sustained by adding pressure in some way. Managing our self and others the way the Lord demonstrated provides a nice foundation for minimizing the problems that can hold back a missionary's performance.

It's Always Best if We Manage Our Self and others According to Priesthood Principles.

Mission leaders who lead according to the priesthood principles discussed above will be more effective in helping those they serve reach their full potential as missionaries. They will not be adding unnecessary frustration and burden to missionaries; which inevitably happens when these principles are not followed. They will be following the Lord's instruction given to early leaders of the Church in the Book of Mormon, "Therefore, what manner of men ought you to be? Verily I say unto you, even as I am" (3 Nephi 27:27).

Of course, these principles also apply equally to how missionaries manage themselves. It's surprising how many missionaries treat themselves in a way that they would never treat others. The famous golden rule taught by the Savior reads, "Therefore all things whatsoever ye would that men should do to you, do ye even so to them: for this is the law and the prophets." (Matthew 7:12). I suspect that the Lord might agree with adding a phrase, "do ye even so to them, *and to yourself*". Sister Donald, who was mentioned at the beginning of this chapter might take note. Until advised otherwise by her Mission President, she tried to keep herself moving by internal threat, criticism and guilt. The result was strong performance initially; followed by a loss of motivation and hope, along with increased health problems. She became a much happier, healthier, and also more productive missionary by working on her shortcomings in the context of persuasion, long-suffering, gentleness, meekness, and love unfeigned.

Essentially, in order to get her motivation back, Sister Donald needed a confidence boost. Thankfully, her Mission President followed the Lord's management style, resulting in increased confidence and increased service. She got that both from her Mission President, and from a spiritual confirmation that he was correct in his observations. The good done, however, would soon have evaporated if she had gone back to beating herself up about her failings. The long-term confidence she needed required that she be more charitable and virtuous in her thinking about herself. As the Lord said, "Let thy bowels also be full of charity towards all men, and to the household of faith, and let virtue garnish thy thoughts unceasingly; *then shall thy confidence wax strong in the presence of God*; and the doctrine of the priesthood shall distill upon thy soul as the dews from heaven" (D&C 121:45, italics added). It's obvious that Sister Donald had been treating herself uncharitably. She was generally very charitable toward others; but definitely not toward herself. Likewise, her thoughts were not garnished with virtue; at least in the sense that her thinking about herself was negative and demeaning. The lack of charity, as well as virtuous (positive and upbeat) thought was robbing her of the confidence that she needed.

Of course, as she became more charitable and upbeat with herself, that did not mean that Sister Donald could ignore the need to improve. Changes needed to be made; but treating herself charitably was actually the best way to improve her performance. Recognizing our faults can be motivating and is an important aspect of humility; but performance will improve faster if there are significantly more positives than negatives in the equation. Certainly this is true when considering behavior change over time. A person who changes behavior due to criticism or the threat of punishment will tend to revert back to old behavior once the threat is gone. Behavior change made for positive reasons tends to last. This fact was recognized in ancient times by both Paul (2 Cor. 7:10) and Mormon (Mormon 2:13). This truth is also recognized by Church leaders in our day and is a theme throughout Preach my Gospel.

Finally, with respect to the issue of treating self and others the way the Lord recommends, this is also a critical factor in improving companion relationships. Following priesthood principles with difficult companions is not easy; but always the best strategy.

Treat Companions According to Priesthood Principles.

Elder Rogers was assigned a difficult companion. In fact, his Mission President suggested beforehand that the assignment might be a challenge; but one he was confident Elder Rogers could handle. After a few days with his new companion, Elder Rogers wasn't so sure. His companion was frequently sullen and angry. He was reluctant to participate in companion study and planning activities; and he was generally negative about whatever the plan was. Interacting with this companion was like walking on eggs. It seemed that no matter what Elder Rogers did, his companion was likely to get upset about it.

Elder Rogers had a patient, charitable personality; and he believed in managing others according to priesthood principles— which is likely why he was selected for this assignment in the first place. However, the frustrating situation he found himself in with this companion stretched his patience to the limit and made him wonder if maybe a little force and coercion might be the right idea after all. As difficult as it was, however, Elder Rogers found several things that helped.

First, he decided to live by priesthood principles no matter what. In other words he would do his best to treat his companion with courtesy and respect even if it didn't seem to make a positive difference; and even if it wasn't fair that he did all of the giving. By doing this, at the end of a difficult day, Elder Rogers was at least able to feel good about himself and give himself credit for doing the right thing.

Second, Elder Rogers invited his companion to understand his needs. Whether it did any good or not, it was important that he give his companion an opportunity to understand his frustration. He did this using an "I" message as opposed to a "you" message. In sending an "I" message, missionaries admit that they have a problem and that they would appreciate their companion's help with it. Conversely, a "you" message indicates that the companion has a problem which he or she needs to work on. "You" messages tend to be manipulative and confrontational; whereas "I" messages are much less so. In line with the advice in Section 121 of the Doctrine and Covenants, "you" messages should be avoided; and even an "I" message should be delivered only when moved upon by the Holy Ghost.

For instance, his companion had been especially negative about the plan for the day and Elder Rogers felt inspired to say, "When you put down the plans I make but won't contribute any ideas of your own, I feel all of the responsibility and that's uncomfortable for me. I would really appreciate your help." Elder Rogers didn't make it a "you" message by saying, "You always put my ideas down but you never make any of your own. You are being ridiculous. We can't be effective missionaries if you continue to act this way."

Even though Elder Rogers did it just right, his companion didn't take it well. Actually, an argument was avoided; which was no small victory; but his companion still became sullen and negative in spite of the less confrontational approach. In fact, he continued to act this way no matter what Elder Rogers did. This meant that the last step for Elder Rogers was to forgive his companion for his unreasonable and frustrating behavior. Elder Rogers did his part by making every effort to understand his companion and to look for the good in him, while minimizing the bad. He kept reminding himself that the problems he was experiencing with his companion were temporary; and that both he and his companion would benefit if Elder Rogers could follow the Savior's example and be charitable and forgiving. Finally, and most importantly, Elder Rogers prayed for help in forgiving his companion; and in so doing, found the strength to do what would otherwise have been extremely difficult, or even impossible.

These are the three steps recommended in any situation with a difficult companion. First, try your best to do the right thing, in spite of how your companion acts. Second, send "I messages" when inspired to do so that specify your problem and request the help of your companion in resolving it. Lastly, every effort needs to be made to forgive your companion and to not let his or her problem become your problem. If the situation is significantly handicapping the missionary work you are doing, you might also take a fourth step by alerting the Mission President of the problem. Other than these steps, the sensible thing is to accept the situation rather than fighting to correct it. Remember that the Lord is aware of what is happening and all of its implications. You now have the opportunity to prove yourself to be a true disciple, even under difficult circumstances.

Of course, all of this is much easier said than done. It's natural when frustrated to become angry; and forgiving unreasonable behavior is a real challenge. Specific suggestions regarding how to manage anger and forgive others are found in the next two chapters.

CHAPTER EIGHT

MISTAKE EIGHT: LETTING ANGER AND FEAR GET OUT OF CONTROL

Anger management skills are definitely tested when serving a mission. Part of the problem, of course, is the tight living quarters and the requirement to stay within sight and sound of one or more companions at all times. Even in marriage, spouses have less intense involvement with one another and much more relief from the idiosyncrasies of their partners. If not handled properly, the stress and strain of missionary service can increase irritability beyond normal limits. Happily, most missionaries handle these stresses with only occasional and relatively minor anger management problems. On the other hand, some missionaries find themselves becoming verbally and even physically abusive. When we first arrived in the Pacific Area to serve as Area Mental Health Advisors, the Area Presidency expressed their concern about this problem, and requested our help in reducing the number of missionaries who had to be released early because they had physically assaulted a companion. Such instances were relatively rare; but very traumatic for everyone concerned when they did happen.

Then too, even occasional and more mundane missionary anger problems can be troubling. Mismanaged anger, even when it falls short of extreme verbal or physical abuse, is still a good way to drive away the Spirit. It can create trust and other relationship issues; not to mention the negative impact persistent anger has on stress levels and general health. Anything missionaries can do while serving to increase their ability to manage anger will pay large dividends while on their mission; and as they go through life.

Anger as Understood From a Scriptural Standpoint

It seems clear in scripture that God too experiences anger. Among many examples, we read in Doctrine and Covenants 5:8, "Oh, this unbelieving and stiff-necked generation—mine anger is kindled against them". As another example of godly anger, there is the well-known instance in which Jesus made a scourge of small cords and drove moneychangers from the temple (John 2:13-17). Anger is apparently part of the divine character; but clearly in the case of God, it is an emotion that is under complete control. It's frightening to think of an omnipotent God who couldn't control his emotions. Which means, of course, that if we are ever to become a joint heir with Christ (Romans 8:17) and receive all that the Father has (D&C 84:38), we too must learn to control anger completely. It's obviously one of those passions that Alma and many other prophets have taught, must be kept within bounds (Alma 38:12).

When this doesn't happen, anger is described in scripture as a curse (Genesis 49:7); or as foolish (Proverbs 27:4). Also in Proverbs, anger is described as cruel and outrageous (Proverbs 27:4). Elsewhere in scripture we are advised to put off or put away anger (Colossians 3:8 and Ephesians 4:31). Along the same lines, as part of the Sermon on the Mount, the Lord himself said the following about anger:

"Ye have heard that it hath been said by them of old time, and it is also written before you, that thou shat not kill, and

162

whosoever shall kill shall be in danger of the judgment of God; But I say unto you, that whosoever is angry with his brother (*without a cause*) shall be in danger of his (*the*) judgment. And whosoever shall say to his brother, Raca, shall be in danger of the council; and whosoever shall say, Thou fool, shall be in danger of hell fire" (3 Nephi 12:21-22; differences found in Matthew 5:21-22 noted in parenthesis and italics).

There are two interesting differences between the Lord's instructions recorded as above in the Book of Mormon, when compared to the account of the same sermon given in Matthew in the New Testament. The two changes are noted above in parenthesis and italics. The Matthew account adds the phrase "without a cause"; and the word "his", as found in the Book of Mormon, becomes a "the" in Matthew.

In the Matthew version, it sounds like we only need to worry about God judging us if we act inappropriately in anger. In fact, as suggested in the Book of Mormon rendering, there are many natural consequences of misplaced anger that will cause us a problem in addition to God's disapproval. These natural consequences flow from misplaced anger whether there is just cause for being angry or not. From this perspective, the added phrase in Matthew "without a cause" is unnecessary, and even misleading.

Taking a life in anger was obviously condemned under the Law of Moses; but under the higher law that the Lord was introducing in the Sermon on the Mount, non-lethal expressions of anger were also condemned. The fact is that, even if we avoid taking a life in anger, whenever anger causes us to act in hurtful or unrighteous ways, there are always unwanted consequences.

First, we can make an enemy of the person to whom our anger is directed, and we are in danger of that person then judging us negatively. Second, others may see our reaction and will likely lose respect for us; and of course, there may be legal implications to our actions in certain cases. Third, we often end up feeling guilty that we reacted as we did and therefore judge ourselves harshly. And finally, we displease God in that we fall short of what He wants us to be. The first three of these consequences correspond to the points made by the Savior quoted in the Book of Mormon account. When we react inappropriately in anger, we are in danger of being judged negatively by the person at whom we are angry (his, not "the" judgment), others (the council) and ourselves (hell fire)*.

As an example of how this can work in missionary life, Elder Hadley was frequently upset by his District Leader's actions; which he perceived to be hypocritical and condemning. The proverbial "last straw" occurred in a District Meeting when the District Leader again said or did something Elder Hadley found offensive. At that point, Elder Hadley blew up and said some very

----

*The expression "hell fire" in scripture often refers to personal torment caused by guilt. As Joseph Smith explained, "A man is his own tormentor and his own condemner. Hence the saying, they shall go into the lake that burns with fire and brimstone. The torment of disappointment in the mind of man is as exquisite as a lake burning with fire and brimstone" (Joseph Fielding Smith, Joseph Smith, *Teachings of the Prophet Joseph Smith*, Deseret Book, 1938, p. 357

unkind things before storming out of the meeting. His companion went after him; but Elder Hadley refused to talk, got in their car and drove off alone.

Think of the consequences of Elder Hadley's actions. His District Leader might have been annoying; but he was not intentionally trying to frustrate Elder Hadley. The District Leader would correctly judge Elder Hadley's actions to be unreasonable and he would lose respect for him. Others in the district who witnessed the outburst would also likely lose respect for Elder Hadley. They might understand the frustration but not the response. His driving off alone would require counselling from his Mission President, who would obviously be concerned about Elder Hadley's behavior.

Then assume that the process of his blowing up, Elder Hadley pushed his companion out of the way, hurting him in the process; or maybe in driving off in anger he damaged property or hurt someone else. Now his priesthood leaders and civil authorities (the council) would officially become involved. Again, the frustration may be understandable, but the response could not be condoned. Finally, at some point, Elder Hadley would likely feel horrible about the incident, and the guilt could be devastating depending on the damage done. There is obvious wisdom in the Lord's instruction to keep anger under control, even when there may be cause for getting upset.

It's Possible to Control Our Anger

When attempting to manage anger, it's helpful to understand its source. From scripture we learn that Lucifer is behind much of the anger we experience.

"For verily, verily I say unto you, he that hath the spirit of contention is not of me, but is of the devil, who is the father of contention, and he stirreth up the hearts of men to contend with anger, one with another.

Behold, this is not my doctrine, to stir up the hearts of men with anger, one against another; but this is my doctrine, that such things should be done away" (3 Nephi 11:29-30).

In these verses, Lucifer is described by the Lord as the father of contention—one who actively stirs the hearts of men to be angry with one another. But how does he do this in practice? He isn't generally an obvious physical presence. That is, we typically don't see him or interact as one person to another. Furthermore, he is not able to force us in any way. (See, for example, 2 Nephi 2 verses 27 and 28 which indicate that we are free to act for ourselves and not to be acted upon.) Or as Joseph Smith succinctly observed, "The devil has no power over us only as we permit him. The moment we revolt at anything which comes from God, the devil takes power" (Joseph Fielding Smith, Joseph Smith, *Teachings of the Prophet Joseph Smith*, Deseret Book, 1938).

Lucifer's influence must amount to enticements to think in certain ways that will then cause anger and contention. In Elder Hadley's case for example, evil would encourage him to focus on how unfair the situation was. Evil would suggest he think how hypocritical his District Leader was, or how picky, or how unreasonable. Elder Hadley would be encouraged to think things like, "I can't stand this"; or "I can't let him get away with treating me this way". On the other hand, the Spirit would suggest he think things like: "No one's perfect. He is trying his best". "No big deal". "It wasn't intentional". "There is no reason to let his problem become my problem". It's obvious the difference in emotion that would result depending on which direction Elder Hadley took in his thinking.

This leads to a very important point. We can choose what we think, but not how we feel. If we want to manage anger, we will have to manage the thoughts that cause anger. We can't just wish or even pray anger away. It will be there, and likely grow, as long as we continue to think in ways that cause or reinforce the emotion. The quicker we can get to positive, or at least neutral thinking, the quicker anger will resolve. Anything we can find that will distract us away from obsessing about the offense will help. Thinking in ways conducive to the Spirit (as in the examples given above) will help. Venting, or giving free rein to angry thoughts will make matters worse.

Contrary to this truth, venting anger is sometimes thought of as a healthy strategy. The theory seems to be that anger builds up like steam in a closed container and must be vented or damage will occur. Of course, this viewpoint is not supported by scripture. Scripture advises that we manage anger in the ways suggested above. We do so by ignoring the temptation to think angry thoughts. When we successfully ignore this temptation and choose a righteous alternative in our thinking, we cut off anger at its source. In that way, anger doesn't build in the first place and we therefore have nothing to suppress.

Brigham Young put it this way:

"When evil arises within me let me throw a cloak over it, subdue it instead of acting it out upon the false presumption that I am honest and no hypocrite.....When my feelings are aroused to anger by the ill-doings of others, I hold them as I would a wild horse, and I gain the victory. Some think and say that it makes them feel better when they are mad, as they call it, to give vent to their madness in abusive and unbecoming language. This, however, is a mistake. Instead of it making you feel better, it is making bad worse. When you think and say it makes you better you give credit to a falsehood. When the wrath and bitterness of the human heart are molded into words and hurled with violence at one another, without any check or hindrance, the fire has no sooner expended itself than it is again re-kindled through some trifling course until the course of nature is set on fire; 'and it is set on fire in hell'" (Journal of Discourses, 26 vols. London: Latter-day Saints' Book Depot, 1854-86, 11:255).

As Brigham Young makes clear, it does no good to vent anger. Rather, the goal is to eliminate angry feelings by making the right choices in how we think; which is an easy concept to understand, but may not be so easy to pull off. Thoughts that induce, grow or maintain anger come in many forms. Some of the more common ones generally fall into the following categories:

1. *Thinking how unfair our situation is.* "Poor me" thoughts provide excellent fuel for anger.
2. *Thinking how unnecessary our suffering is.* Dwelling on how whatever offended us never should have

happened will encourage anger. So will thinking how easily the problem could have been avoided if so and so (or I) had just done things a little differently.

3. *Dwelling on the weaknesses and shortcomings of whoever offended us.* Dwelling on how careless, stupid, insensitive, unforgiving, or just outright evil the person who offended us is also results in growing and maintaining anger. This is most likely one of the reasons why so much in scripture warns against judging others.

4. *Thinking in absolutes is a problem.* Thinking in terms of "always", "never", "can't" and "have to" maintain anger. "He *always* does this". "She will *never* change". "I *can't* let him get away with this". "I *have to* get even".

5. *Rehearsing what you would like to say to the offender and/or imagining what you would like to see happen to him.* When offended, it's common to rehearse the speech you want to give to the offender and/or day dream about some form of retaliation. Doing so is an excellent way to grow and foster anger.

6. *Thinking unforgiving thoughts.* "I will never forgive him for what he did." "I won't let him get away with this." Having an unforgiving attitude or thinking unforgiving thoughts will feed anger. The principle of forgiveness is the subject of the next chapter.

7. *Believing that your anger is inevitable or justified.* We sometimes excuse ourselves by blaming someone or something for our anger. "He made me angry" or "I couldn't help it." Managing anger as the scriptures

direct must begin with accepting responsibility for what we are feeling and realizing that it is the natural consequence of what we choose to think.

8. *Denying that we are angry.* Another problem that will keep anger alive and well is to deny that we are angry in the first place. We must recognize and own the emotion before we will have much luck managing it. This can be a particular problem with passive aggressive responses. A missionary may not recognize an anger problem because he or she doesn't yell, scream, or hit walls. Withdrawn, sullen, or manipulative behavior can still push away the Spirit and cause interpersonal and health problems.

When any of these thought patterns are recognized, or when you feel anger building for any reason, you might find value in the following suggestions:

1. *Pray for help in forgiving and distracting.* As mentioned earlier, you can't pray anger away if you continue to think in ways that sustain and grow your angry feelings. At the same time, doing our part to manage anger by distracting ourselves and reformulating our thinking is easier said than done. Thankfully, divine help is available, and is often necessary, in effective anger management.

2. *Calm Down*
   a. Where possible, move away from the irritating situation. Take time out. The part of your brain that creates an angry

feeling is quicker to respond than the part
of your brain that can reason and make
good decisions. Find a way to give
yourself time for the reasoning and good
judgement to kick in.

b. Take a deep breath, or a series of them.
Tell yourself you are not going to let
whatever you are concerned about matter.

c. Count backwards, sing a hymn, and recite
a favourite forgiveness scripture (i.e.
D&C 64: 8-10); or distract your thinking
by focusing on something other than the
issue that is annoying you.

d. Think peaceful thoughts. DO NOT
review the problem in your mind.

3. *Rethink the situation.*

a. Remember that in the longer term
whatever you are mad about doesn't
really matter. The only thing that
matters is how you respond to
provocation.

b. Consciously decide to let the other
person get away with it and then think
about something else. Don't dwell on
the problem.

c. Literally count your many blessings and
think about the good things in your life.

d. Remember that the Lord requires of us
to manage our anger; and He does not

require anything that is not possible. (1 Nephi 3:7)

4. *Look for triggers of your anger and think of ways to avoid them.*

    a. Don't think about or try to handle frustrating things or people when you are hungry, angry, frustrated, stressed out or tired.

    b. Try to think more positively about people/situations that frustrate you. Yes, there are obvious problems; but what is good about him/her or the situation?

    c. Avoid thinking in absolutes.

5. *Be willing to apologize, serve, and try to understand those who trigger your anger.*

    a. Look in the mirror when you are angry. You may not like what you see.

    b. Take the higher road by being willing to apologize. Genuinely ask for what you can do to make things right.

    c. Follow the direction from the Lord to "do good to them that hate you, and pray for them who despitefully use you and persecute you" (3 Nephi 12:44).

6. *Keep an anger log.* For one week, record the "trigger events" that seemed to spark your anger, what you were angry about, and how you handled the anger. Based on your findings, prayerfully develop a plan for

how to handle the "trigger events" differently next time.

7. *Learn constructive ways of dealing with problems.*

    a. Ask for what you want, but don't insist or demand.

    b. Own the problem rather than blaming/attacking the other person. Find ways to solve the problem on your own where possible; and decide not to worry about it when that isn't possible.

    c. Try to understand the other person. Ask specific questions to check your conclusions about the other person; e.g., "It sounds like you think I am an idiot. Is that what you really meant to say?"

    d. As described in Chapter Three, use the magic words, "You might be right" when you disagree with someone; or when they disagree with you.

    e. Work for a "win/win" solution when your opinions or wishes conflict with others. It's almost always possible to reach a compromise that works for everyone when all parties involved are sufficiently humble and forgiving. Of course, you can't guarantee that someone else will be humble and forgiving; but you can insure that you are.

It should also be noted that anger management is closely related to a number of general gospel principles. When we are angry at someone else, the usual tendency is to think of all of their shortcomings. We can clearly see that they are being prideful, intolerant or whatever. It works a lot better to focus on our virtue or lack thereof instead. For example, we might ask our self, am I sufficiently humble in this relationship; or do I insist that I am right and that my opinion must be respected? Am I being patient and tolerant? I don't have to go to unreasonable lengths, but am I being unselfish; and am I willing to serve others, even though they seem to be disrespecting me? Am I being self-centered or am I honestly trying to see the problem through the others' eyes?

Am I thinking about the other charitably; and perhaps most important of all, am I sufficiently forgiving? The need to become really good at forgiving others is the subject of the next chapter.

Missionaries Need to Learn How to Manage Fear (Anxiety)

As the preceding discussion has hopefully made clear, it's necessary that missionaries, and all of us for that matter, learn to manage anger. Missionary work can be challenging in this regard; but at the same time, it also provides a great opportunity to develop this important skill. There is likewise another natural emotion that needs to be managed in order to have a successful mission and life. That is the emotion of fear. The ability that our brains have to provide an automatic and immediate alarm response can literally save us by causing us to jump out of the way of a falling boulder; or give us maximum strength and alertness in a time of danger. More general fear, such as the fear of displeasing God or others, can motivate missionaries to do hard things and to put greater

174

effort into worthwhile goals. On the other hand, intense fear is immobilizing. It can destroy initiative and strangle effectiveness. From an emotional and mental health standpoint, unmanaged fear results in anxiety, post-traumatic stress, panic attacks, and phobias. A significant percentage of missionaries who are unable to complete their service suffer from these kinds of fear-related issues.

The goal, of course, is to take advantage of the positive benefits of fear and to avoid the negative. Or in other words, fear is another passion that needs to be kept within bounds. Problems associated with anxiety, panic attacks, and other mental health fear-related issues can be managed as described below. The negative consequences of general fear can be managed by developing faith and thinking about the world in a healthy way. This seems to be what President Hinckley was referring to when he said the following:

"Who among us can say that he or she has not felt fear? I know of no one who has been entirely spared. Some, of course, experience fear to a greater degree than do others. Some are able to rise above it quickly, but others are trapped and pulled down by it and even driven to defeat. We suffer from the fear of ridicule, the fear of failure, the fear of loneliness, the fear of ignorance. Some fear the present, some the future. Some carry the burden of sin and would give almost anything to unshackle themselves from those burdens but fear to change their lives. Let us recognize that fear comes not of God but rather that this gnawing, destructive element comes from the adversary of truth and righteousness. Fear is the antithesis of faith. It is corrosive in its effects, even deadly" (Gordon B. Hinckley, "God Hath Not Given Us the Spirit of Fear" *Ensign*, Oct. 1984, 2).

Here we have a modern prophet spelling it out for us. Excessive fear is unnecessary and destructive. It's on the list of common temptations designed to upset us and take us off track. President Hinckley was, of course, alluding to general fear that is misplaced or extreme. This kind of fear results from lacking sufficient faith in God and His plan. The good news is that the intense involvement missionaries have in scripture study, prayer and service are all the very things that build faith. Most missionaries will find that investing fully in their mission and being obedient to mission rules will reduce unwanted general fear dramatically. As indicated below, some of the emotional/mental health implications of unmanaged fear, however, take a somewhat different approach to resolve.

Managing Anxiety and Panic Attacks.

Elder Marsh had some trouble with anxiety and minor panic attacks during his high school years; but nothing like the experience he had flying from his home to the MTC in New Zealand. As he was sitting on the airplane, he was surprised by an overwhelming sense of panic that seemed to come out of nowhere. His heart started racing and he began to have a hard time breathing. He noticed he was sweating and shaking and then he began to feel an intense pain in his chest. He really thought he was dying. His condition was obvious to those around him and flight attendants got involved and moved him to a seat by himself where they administered oxygen and finally got him stabilized somewhat.

However, he remained very uncomfortable for the remainder of the flight. On landing, medical personnel met him at the gate and took him to a local hospital. To say the least, this was not the beginning to his mission that he had anticipated.

Tests at the hospital found no physical problems with his heart or anything else; and he was soon released and moved to the MTC. There the Area Mental Health Advisor checked in with him and together they were able to determine what had happened and how to deal with this kind of experience if it were to happen again. Elder Marsh was quite worried about that possibility since he was scheduled to get on another airplane and fly four hours to his mission assignment in two weeks.

Here is what Elder Marsh learned. For some reason-- perhaps his excitement and concern about the MTC and his mission; or maybe he got to thinking that he was trapped in a metal tube 35,000 feet in the air--the part of his brain that automatically responds to threat was triggered. That part of the brain then caused a release of chemicals into his system which increased his heart rate, breathing rate, and changed the distribution of blood flow in his body. Lack of oxygen to chest muscles, the fact that his chest muscles were being overworked, or other reasons explained by his physiology, likely accounted for the intense chest pain.

The part of his brain causing this reaction is a part of all normal brains and kicks into gear automatically when threat is perceived. Unfortunately, the response can be triggered in some cases when there is actually no threat; or when the threat is perceived but not real. It also seems to trigger more easily, and it will create a more dramatic reaction, in some people than in others.

For whatever reason it happens and to whatever degree, however, once the reaction is triggered, our conscious brain gets involved. At that point, the direction we take in our thinking determines whether the automatic response continues or is turned off. In Elder Marsh's case, he kept thinking things like, "I'm dying", "I'm embarrassing myself and the Church", "Something is terribly wrong", and "Why aren't my prayers being answered?" (he was praying fervently for relief but the panic seemed to deepen)". Thinking this way obviously reinforced the sense of danger and the automatic part of his brain therefore continued to release stress chemicals into his system.

Once the general mechanics causing his symptoms were understood, Elder Marsh, of course, then wanted to know how to turn this reaction off. There are actually several things that will cause this automatic response in the brain to shut off. The first is distraction.

Distraction can help the brain reset once a panic response is initiated. Suppose that as Elder Marsh first began to notice the panic symptoms, the person in the seat next to him started choking and was turning blue. What would have happened to Elder Marsh's panic symptoms? Most likely, the medical emergency next to him would catch his complete attention. He would no longer be thinking thoughts that kept his state of alarm alive; and his brain would have automatically reset. Extreme panic symptoms would then have magically disappeared. The tendency when experiencing panic is to fight it; or to put concentration and energy into solving the problem. Usually all this does is make things worse. The much better strategy is to focus on issues outside of oneself.

As another analogy, if non-swimmers are plunged into deep water, they tend to fight to stay afloat. If they can contradict this normal reaction by distracting themselves from thinking about the danger; and if they can relax their body, they will have a much better chance of survival. Granted, it's hard to think of something else when facing what appears to be a life-threatening situation; but it is generally possible, especially when the situation is understood. Which suggests that the first thing to do when experiencing a panic attack is to label it. "Ah, this is a panic attack. It feels horrible but I know I am in no danger".

In terms of how to distract ourselves, anything that can grab our attention will do. Sometimes changing the venue can help in this regard. Assuming conditions allowed, Elder Marsh might have gotten up and walked around the airplane; or he could have gone to the bathroom and splashed a little water on his face. Just the process of changing locations might have helped him think of something else. It's also a great distraction to get into a conversation with someone. Again, if circumstances had allowed, and Elder Marsh had gotten into a discussion with a seat mate, the panic might not have registered and/or it would have reset quickly. Naturally, as a brand new missionary, a gospel discussion with his seat mate would have been a wonderful distraction and a great start to his mission. Brain teasers, reciting scriptures, singing songs, planning a talk, solving a problem, writing a letter, or any number of other distractions were also available to Elder Marsh.

Deep breathing exercises can help the brain reset when a panic reaction is initiated. It takes the conscious brain a bit of time to have an impact on the automatic part of the brain. On the other hand, deep breathing can send an "all clear" signal more immediately. If Elder Marsh had sat back in his airline seat, closed his eyes, and taken several deep breaths, it's likely his panic symptoms would have disappeared—especially if he was able to distract his thinking away from himself; and away from how his body was responding. In terms of the specifics of what he might have done, the breathing exercise described in the *Adjusting to Missionary Life* resource booklet referred to earlier (page 18) could have been a great help.

1. Sit in a comfortable position or stand quietly. Take a few deep, slow breaths through your nose, pausing after each one.
2. Relax your shoulders and try to breathe so your stomach moves, not your shoulders.
3. Continue to breathe slowly and calmly for five minutes or until anxious feelings ease up.

Deep breathing exercises like the one just described are most effective if practiced. Someone prone to panic attacks or extreme anxiety, or any of us for that matter, can benefit by spending a few minutes several times a day doing this simple exercise. This can help train the body to relax more quickly when an anxiety response is triggered.

A progressive relaxation exercise can also be helpful. In addition to the breathing exercise just mentioned, the following relaxation exercise found in the *Adjusting to Missionary Life* resource booklet (page 19) might also have helped.

1. Lie or sit comfortably and close your eyes.
2. Concentrating on one part of your body at a time, look for any tension. Consciously relax that part of your

body. Feel all the tension draining away, like sand running through your fingers. Then move on to the next part of your body. Take your time. If you are not sure if there is still tension, tighten that part of your body for 10 seconds; then completely relax for 10 seconds before moving on.

3. Focus on these areas, one at a time: 1. head and face; 2. eyes; 3. jaw; 4. neck; 5. shoulders and back; 6. arms; 7. hands and fingers, 8. chest and abdomen; 9. legs; 10. feet and toes.

4. Mentally scan your body for any remaining tension. Completely relax.

5. Choose a "personal scene"—a memory or an imagined setting—that brings you joy and peace. Try to imagine the scene as vividly as possible.

Slow, measured breathing, and relaxed muscles send an all-clear signal that will cause the automatic part of the brain to reset.

Drugs can also reset the switch and stop a panic response. Certain drugs will directly impact the automatic response in the brain and shut down a panic response. However, since the drugs that do this have the potential to be habit forming, they are generally not the best option for solving anxiety or panic problems. In some cases, these drugs have been approved for short term use by missionaries; but they are monitored carefully and used only when necessary. Often, in fact, just having medication available is all that is needed. Knowing that they have a pill available just in case allows a missionary to not worry when symptoms are noticed; and they are then in a better position to follow the suggestions for helping the brain reset as described above.

From his experience, Elder Marsh learned that he is not at the mercy of his body when anxiety and panic are triggered. He took comfort in having a plan involving the following steps that he could take when and if the problem ever came up again.

1. If he noticed symptoms starting, he would remind himself that he knew what this was; and that he was in no danger. Actually, the worst thing that can happen physically during a panic attack is that someone might not get enough oxygen to the brain and pass out. Normally, this would be a brief period of unconsciousness during which the brain would reset and the person would awake without the panic feelings.
2. Elder Marsh would put effort into focusing on something outside of himself. He would say a short prayer emphasizing his gratitude for his many blessings and asking for help in getting his mind on something positive. He would then involve himself in a conversation with someone else, get up and walk around, or do any number of other things that would be distracting.
3. As appropriate, he would also do the deep breathing and progressive relaxation exercise described above.

Thus armed with a plan, Elder Marsh was able to get on the airplane after his brief MTC training; and he arrived at his mission headquarters without incident. He then went on to serve admirably and was over a year into his mission at the time of this writing.

Managing emotion effectively, especially anger and fear, are a big part of the equation in effective missionary work. As discussed in the next chapter, forgiveness is one of the more powerful principles of the gospel that can help us control anger and other unwanted emotions.

CHAPTER NINE

MISTAKE NINE: NOT BEING QUICK TO FORGIVE

Forgiveness is one of the most beneficial principles taught in scripture, yet one we often have trouble applying. It's certainly a principle that missionaries have many opportunities to practice. Some have major offenses to forgive. For example, a sister missionary in Tahiti was riding her bicycle when a drunk driver swerved off the road and hit her. She suffered severe brain trauma and other injuries and was not expected to live. Through a series of miracles, she was healed to the point that she was able to return to her mission within a few months. On her return to Tahiti, she was able to meet the man who had so severely injured her. She had early on been able to frankly forgive the man; and now she had the chance to express her forgiveness personally. Her doing so was a tremendous blessing to the man guilty of almost taking her life; but it was also a great blessing to the missionary. Part of the reason behind her miraculous recovery may be the fact that her spirit and will were not handicapped by hate for the man who had caused her injury; nor did she spend a lot of time bemoaning how unfair her situation was.

Most missionaries, however, will not have such major offenses to forgive. Their challenge will be the little frustrations, the minor offenses that come up almost every day; which can sometimes be the bigger test. For instance, your companion makes a critical comment about you. A ward member fails to follow through on something important that was promised. Your companion left a mess for you to clean up. The Zone Leader is putting pressure on you to do better when you are already doing the best you can. A false rumor has been circulated about you among the missionaries. A member complains about your language skills in spite of your great effort to learn his difficult language. And on and on it goes. Often in cases of minor offense, we feel justified in our feelings and actions and don't even see the need to forgive. Yet, forgiving is still required. It's the quickest, and often the only way to insure peace of mind, and to avoid damaging our relationships with others. It's often a requirement if we are to handle even routine life events effectively.

Whether the offense is great or small, taking the high road and forgiving an offense is always in our best interest. This can be stated emphatically because we have the word of the Lord on it.

What Scripture Suggests

One of the many references in scripture regarding the need to forgive others is the powerful statement made by the Lord in the Doctrine and Covenants.

"My disciples, in days of old, sought occasion against one another and forgave not one another in their hearts; and for this evil they were afflicted and sorely chastened.

Wherefore I say unto you, that ye ought to forgive one another; for he that forgiveth not his brother his trespasses standeth condemned before the Lord; for there remaineth in him the greater sin.

I the Lord, will forgive whom I will forgive, but of you it is required to forgive all men" (D&C 64:8-10).

It's interesting to note that the Savior in this scripture is describing disciples. These were early missionaries and people of faith, who were committed to him; yet who found reasons to be upset with each other, and who failed to forgive. It's also worth noting that they failed to forgive one another "in their hearts". Perhaps they were able to forgive intellectually, but emotionally (in their hearts) they were still holding a grudge. Finally, because of this they were afflicted and sorely chastened.

It's probable that this chastening didn't come from God in any direct way, but rather represented the natural consequences of failing to forgive. As most of us well know, failing to forgive leads to uncomfortable and unproductive emotions within ourselves, and it leads to significant pain interpersonally. It can also have eternal implications. As the Lord said, "But if ye forgive not men their trespasses, neither will your Father forgive you your trespasses (Matthew 6:15). Likely, this is because failing to forgive reveals a personal callousness; and in effect, a denial of the atonement--neither of which can be tolerated in the celestial world. As President Uchtdorf has taught, "Because we all depend on mercy from God, how can we deny to others any measure of the grace we so desperately desire for ourselves?" (Dieter F. Uchtdorf, "The Merciful Obtain Mercy", *Ensign*, May 2012).

In the last verse of the scripture quoted above, the Lord indicates that we are to forgive *all* men; which includes even those who don't deserve our forgiveness. Among this group are those who are not repentant, and those who seem to glory in our suffering. Offenders will face the judgment of God, and He will forgive who He will. We, however, must forgive everyone. Why? Again, most likely because doing so is in our best interest. It is good medicine in the here and now as well as an eternal requirement. Perhaps it isn't so much a test of faith, or some hurdle we must jump over to prove ourselves to God. But rather, like all commandments, it may be a rule given for our protection and advantage—both here and in the hereafter. Also, our ability to forgive depends on virtues such as tolerance, patience, and charity that are essential in a celestial person. Unforgiving individuals who have not developed these qualities will not be able to abide a celestial glory.

No matter whoever or whatever the object of our forgiving, the act of forgiving results in great blessings; while failing to forgive guarantees significant negative consequences. That could be why the Lord also points out, in the scripture quoted above, that our not forgiving is a worse sin than the one we fail to forgive. In terms of the young missionary mentioned earlier who was hit by a drunk driver, if she had failed to forgive the man who hit her, on any reasonable moral scale, the man's sin would obviously still be much greater than hers. Why then would the Lord tell us that, if she failed to forgive, her sin would be the greater? The answer might lie in the fact that the missionary was not guilty of any crime. This means that failing to forgive is the worst sin in this situation, *for which she would be accountable*. It's the only moral mistake that she could make that would add unnecessarily to her suffering. In this sense, failing to forgive would truly be the worst sin as far as she is concerned.

Additional Scripture

> "Then came Peter to him, and said, Lord, how oft shall my brother sin against me, and I forgive him? Till seven times?

> Jesus saith unto him, I say not unto thee, Until seven times; but, Until seventy times seven" (Matthew 18:21-22).

In these verses the Lord indicates that we should continually forgive no matter how often an offense is repeated. The need to forgive an offender over and over becomes an issue primarily with respect to relatively small offenses from people with whom we have a close relationship. In missionary service, this most often involves a companion.

Sister Lupe had this challenge. Her companion was not as dedicated to her mission as she should be. Sister Lupe, on the other hand, was fully engaged and wanted to use every minute of her service productively. This difference in attitude and commitment caused frustration multiple times a day. For instance, Sister Lupe was frustrated when she was forced to wait for her companion to get ready; when she had to study alone because her companion refused to participate in companion study; or when her companion developed a "headache" after a few minutes of a finding activity and insisted on returning to their flat. These kinds of things happened regularly and repeatedly.

Although it was difficult, Sister Lupe was able to be forgiving at first; but that became increasingly difficult as these kinds of incidents occurred over and over again. Sister Lupe asked for cooperation from her companion, even pleading that she get with the program; but to no avail. Not only did her companion continue to frustrate her repeatedly; she didn't seem to be concerned. In fact, she was frequently critical of Sister Lupe for being insensitive to her "health needs"; and she claimed that Sister Lupe was self-righteous and obsessive in her efforts to be the perfect missionary. Finally, Sister Lupe had reached the limit of her tolerance and she blew up at her companion saying everything and more that she had been thinking for some time; but which she had so far managed not to say. The result was a disaster for both her companion, who now blamed Sister Lupe for her critical comments along with everything else; and for Sister Lupe, who felt bad for what she had said and the way she had said it.

Sister Lupe's frustration was understandable. She really was trying to do the right thing, whereas her companion was clearly not measuring up to her responsibilities. Unfortunately, however, Sister Lupe's failing to forgive was a mistake for which only she was responsible; and one that cost her dearly. In effect, Sister Lupe was a double victim. It was unfair that she had to deal with an uncommitted companion and all the associated problems that came with that fact; however, she was an innocent victim in this regard. On the other hand, the anger and frustration that continued and grew within her resulted from her failing to forgive; which was Sister Lupe's responsibility. She couldn't do anything about being a victim in the first instance; but by forgiving her companion, she could have avoided becoming a double victim.

The need to forgive in situations like this may seem unfair; but it is clearly an important part of our mortal experience. From these kinds of experiences come opportunities to develop the tolerant, long-suffering and charitable nature required in celestial beings. It also usually proves the best way to have a positive impact on others. As the prophet Joseph Smith said, "Nothing is so much calculated to lead people to forsake sin as to take them by the hand and to watch over them in tenderness. When persons manifest the least kindness and love to me, O what power it has over my mind" (Joseph Fielding Smith, Joseph Smith, *Teachings of the Prophet Joseph Smith*, Deseret Book, 1938, p. 240). If there is anything that Sister Lupe might have done that would have helped her companion step up to her responsibilities, it would be to continue being the best missionary she could be under the circumstances; while at the same time treating her companion kindly. It doesn't always work; but there are many cases where a reluctant partner does come around eventually if treated well in spite of how undeserving he or she might be at first.

Why Is It So Hard?

Sister Lupe made several common mistakes that made forgiving her companion more difficult than it needed to be. For one thing, she compounded issues by taking her companion's negative behavior personally. She assumed that her companion hated her and didn't respect her. Although untrue, this conclusion was especially difficult to handle emotionally. Sister Lupe also made a second mistake by assuming that the negative impact her companion's behavior had on their missionary work meant that she was failing as a missionary. This was likewise not true. Sister Lupe was doing the best she could under the circumstances; and she was not responsible for the fact that they were falling short of their potential. Incorrectly perceiving the situation as she did made this a much bigger issue than it needed to be; thus making it more difficult to forgive.

Sister Lupe also felt like she had to continually make a point about her companion's lack of commitment. Whenever the problem came up, she felt obligated to say something, or act in a negative way, in order to avoid seeming to condone her partner's behavior. At the same time, Sister Lupe understood the need to be forgiving and avoid criticism. This conflict put an unnecessary emotional burden on Sister Lupe. It's very hard to forgive if we consider forgiving to be, in effect, condoning or reinforcing the behavior that offends us.

Additionally, Sister Lupe needed things to be fair. Here she was doing the right thing and her companion was not; yet, her companion seemed to be getting away with it. She had a good relationship with many of the other missionaries; and the members and investigators seemed to enjoy her laid back, easy-going style. And in spite of the relatively frequent "headaches" and her complaints about Sister Lupe, not much seemed to bother her companion. As a matter of fact, it often looked like she was happier than Sister Lupe. The need to even the scales, and insure fairness, became an obstacle to Sister Lupe's forgiving.

As yet another common mistake, Sister Lupe had become so focused on what bothered her about her companion that she overlooked her companion's strengths. She would deny it if accused, but she had come to see her companion as a person basically incapable of doing the right thing. It's hard to forgive someone if we can't look past their faults and see their redeeming qualities.

Finally, when it came to the relationship she had with her companion, Sister Lupe had effectively blocked herself from the influence of the Spirit. Her unforgiving thoughts about her companion resulted in her being unable to hear the message of the Spirit. She was not able to hear the Spirit confirming how much the Lord loved her and respected her faithful commitment. She was not able to feel the comfort in doing the right thing that she might otherwise have felt; and she wasn't able to receive the direction she would have received regarding how to better handle this difficult situation.

The factors identified above that made this an especially difficult challenge for Sister Lupe were largely within her control. Following is a summary of what Sister Lupe, and all of us for that matter, need to remember when facing a need to forgive.

1. *Take the offense at face value rather than reading major issues into it.* The offenses we need to forgive are hard enough to deal with even if we don't read unwarranted conclusions into the situation. Unless there is solid evidence of the fact, it does no good to take offenses personally, or to assume responsibility for someone else's problem. Nor is it helpful to exaggerate the consequences of the offense.

2. *Decide to do the right thing even if the other person seems to be getting away with something they shouldn't.* We need to stay committed to doing the right thing—even if doing so seems to reinforce the offender's behavior. This requires faith that doing the right thing will always work best in the long run.

3. *Do the right thing and leave justice to God.* It sometimes makes sense to confront those who offend us, as discussed later; but no good ever comes from

thinking how unfair the situation is, lecturing or attacking those who offend us, or requiring justice. All of that needs to be left to the Lord.

4. *Look for the good in whoever offends us.* This doesn't mean to naively overlook the bad and continue to expose ourselves to abuse. It just means to recognize the good in a way that will help us have a forgiving attitude.

5. *Call on God for help.* Forgiving another, especially if they are unrepentant, can be a challenge; and we often need spiritual help to pull it off. Some who need to forgive report a long and unsuccessful struggle until they finally humble themselves and call on God in faith and sincerity for help. In many cases they are then gifted with a cleansing of their heart that they were unable to accomplish on their own.

When Have We Truly Forgiven?

Some missionaries claim that they have forgiven another, yet there is good evidence to the contrary. Forgiveness seems to involve two components—how we treat those who have offended us, and how we feel about them. How we should treat those who offend us is made clear in scripture.

"But I say unto you, Love your enemies, bless them that curse you, do good to them that hate you and pray for them which despitefully use you, and persecute you" (Matthew 5:44).

Elder Cummings had a particularly bad experience with a companion along the lines of Sister Lupe's experience with her companion. Things deteriorated to the point that Elder Cummings and his companion had to be separated prior to the next scheduled transfer. Once separated, Elder Cummings was generally able to forget about his former companion and no longer experienced the angry feelings that had consumed him while they were still together. He assumed that the absence of anger meant that he had forgiven his former companion and that all was good. But, in fact, he still had work to do. He was still prone to making negative comments about his former companion whenever the subject came up. And he would ignore his former companion and treat him rudely whenever they ran across each other. Elder Cummings forgiveness would not be complete until he was able to consistently avoid speaking negatively of his former companion; and until he was able to treat him kindly.

Elder Cummings also had some work to do on the second part of what it means to forgive. With his former companion out of sight, he had no problem. But angry feelings were still present whenever he saw him; or the subject of his former companion came up in conversation. As suggested in the Doctrine and Covenants verses quoted earlier, like the disciples of old, Elder Cummings had not forgiven his former companion in his heart (D&C 64:8). His forgiveness wouldn't be complete until he could be in the presence of his former companion, or even just think about him, without experiencing emotional upset.

As a general summary, the following are keys to knowing when we may still have the need to forgive; and/or when our forgiveness is not complete.

1. *When we say or do hurtful things directed toward someone who has offended us.* For example, gossiping about someone who has offended us, treating them rudely, or undermining them in any way.

2. *When we can't feel at ease thinking about, or when in the presence of someone who has offended us.* It's an unnecessary complication in our life when our emotions are under the control of someone else. If we can't be at peace when we think about someone who has offended us, or if we can't be comfortable in their presence, they are in effect, controlling our emotions—which is solid evidence that we have still not completely forgiven them.

3. *When we can't look past offensive behavior for fear of reinforcing or appearing to condone it.* As suggested earlier, doing the right thing may appear to let other people get away with bad behavior. According to the Lord, it is still in everyone's best interest if we do the right thing, no matter the apparent consequences.

4. *When we require justice or demand fairness.* We can seek for fairness and justice by confronting an offender privately in the case of more minor offenses and through outside authorities in the case of serious matters. But we will likely frustrate ourselves and make everything worse if we *demand* justice and fairness. In other words, it's reasonable to seek justice, but a problem if we need it. After basic and reasonable effort on our part to secure justice, justice needs to be left in the hands of the Lord. Forgiveness

needs to be with absolutely no strings attached on our part.

Confronting an Offender

"And if thy brother or sister offend thee, thou shalt take him or her between him or her and thee alone; and if he or she confess thou shalt be reconciled" (D & C 42:88).

It's often best to simply forgive and move on; but there are times when it helps to confront an offender—especially in close and ongoing relationships, such as missionary companionships. In those cases, saying "ouch" when our toes are stepped on has potential advantages—at least assuming we are giving feedback and not attacking the one offending us. For one thing, the person offending may have no clue that we have been offended. When that's the case, it's especially important to bring up our complaint in order to give the offender a clear opportunity to make things right. Confronting someone who upsets us also provides an opportunity to understand the situation in a way we might not have otherwise. For example, in talking through a problem, it might become clear that we have misjudged the other person's actions or motives. In general, talking through our grievances, again if done in the right way, has the potential to build a stronger and more comfortable relationship.

Following the advice in the scripture quoted above, when we bring up a problem, it's important to confront in private. Doing so shows respect for the person confronted; and it increases the likelihood of open communication. Furthermore, it avoids a situation in which someone might be judged, perhaps unfairly, by others who hear about the problem.

Obviously, when we confront someone who has offended us, the situation also has to be handled well, or it will just make things worse. Along with doing so in private, many of the principles discussed in earlier chapters are critical to a successful outcome. For example, any confrontation needs to be in the form of an "I" and not a "you" message; i.e., "I have a problem and I would like your help with it"; not "you have a problem and you had better get it fixed". There also needs to be a strong element of humility. The message needs to be along the lines of "I may be wrong, but this is how I see it"; not "you are wrong and this won't work until you get it right". Finally, following the advice in Section 121 of the Doctrine and Covenants (v. 41-43), the message needs to conveyed in a spirit of kindness, gentleness, meekness, and love unfeigned with an increased show of love afterward (v. 41-42). Any sense of manipulation, control, or personal condemnation will likely result in argument and stalemate.

Putting this into practice, Sister Rawlings learned that a former companion was badmouthing her to others in the mission. Sister Rawlings first option was to overlook the problem and forgive her former companion. This would make sense since gossips often hurt their own reputation more than they do the person they are gossiping about. And anyone who knew Sister Rawlings would judge her on the basis of their own experience, not what they heard about her third hand. In fact, forgiving and moving on would likely be the best option in this situation. If, however, there was a potential for an ongoing relationship with her former companion; and/or if Sister Rawlings was so inspired, then confronting her former companion would be the best choice. This might be one of those "if moved upon by the Holy Ghost" moments; in which case, there would obviously be good reason to confront her offender.

Assuming that to be the case, in order to follow the direction in scripture, Sister Rawlings would need to arrange for a private conversation with her former companion. Her approach would need to be non-confrontational, and follow the suggestions given above. She might say something like, "I hope it's not true, but I have heard that you have been telling others what an uptight, impossible-to-get-along-with person I am. I was hoping our problems were behind us and we could both move on and respect each other. Can we talk about this?" Sister Rawlings would *not* say something like "Look, you've been badmouthing me in the mission and this has to stop! You have no right to say this stuff about me!" Nor would she threaten and try to manipulate her former companion. "If this doesn't stop, I'm going to tell the Mission President exactly what's going on!" Or, "I'm going to make sure everyone knows what you're really like!" An angry and confrontational approach is a common "natural man" response; but clearly, taking the higher road has advantages.

Should the problem continue after her attempt to clearly voice her concern, Sister Rawlings would be left with no option but to forgive her former companion and move on. Trying to get even, worrying about the problem, or trying to force her former companion to cease and desist would all backfire—not to mention cause Sister Rawlings to miss a great opportunity to further develop the pure love of Christ in her heart.

How to Forgive

From the previous discussion, it's hopefully clear why forgiveness is critically important to success both as a missionary; and in our lives generally. Hopefully what it means to forgive and how to know when we have successfully forgiven is also evident. There is still the question, however, regarding how to forgive others. What is the process involved? Following are several ideas that might help.

Forgive by increasing our love for God. President Uchtdorf, in the conference address referenced earlier, taught that we forgive others by developing the love of God within ourselves. "The more we allow the love of God to govern our minds and emotions—the more we allow our love for our Heavenly Father to swell within our hearts—the easier it is to love others with the pure love of Christ…The pure love of Christ can remove the scales of resentment and wrath from our eyes, allowing us to see others the way our Heavenly Father sees us: as flawed and imperfect mortals who have potential and worth far beyond our capacity to imagine. Because God loves us so much, we too must love and forgive each other" (Dieter F. Uchtdorf, "The Merciful Obtain Mercy", *Ensign*, May 2012).

As President Uchtdorf suggests, the pure love of Christ eliminates rancor, hate, and any degree of animosity. Rather than focus on the faults and shortcomings of those who offend us, focusing on our indebtedness to God and building our love and respect for the Savior will allow us to be truly forgiving. In other words, when we experience anger and resentment, rather than focusing on the offender and trying hard to forgive in some direct way, it might be more effective in some cases to focus on the Savior and His atonement. As we let appreciation and love for the Savior grow within us, anger and resentment toward others will diminish naturally.

Monitor and stop unforgiving thoughts. A second strategy in forgiving others involves being aware of our unforgiving thoughts and replacing them. Practically, this brings us back to the ADD strategy explained in earlier chapters. We must become aware (A) when we are thinking negative, unforgiving thoughts about someone. Then we make a decision (D) that this is not what we want to think. This decision is followed immediately by distraction (D)—meaning that we move our thinking to something positive. It usually works best when distracting to think about something unrelated to the offender and the incident that has upset us. Trying to convince ourselves that we need to forgive or forcing kind thoughts about someone who has offended us can work short term; but we are still thinking about the incident. Sooner or later, negative thoughts are likely to return. It usually works best to completely change the subject in our minds.

Refuse to retaliate and where possible, do something nice for those who offend us. Elder Holland shared the following story in one of his conference addresses: "…a sister missionary recently wrote to me: 'My companion and I saw a man sitting on a bench in the town square eating his lunch. As we drew near, he looked up and saw our missionary name tags. With a terrible look in his eye, he jumped up and raised his hand to hit me. I ducked just in time, only to have him spit his food all over me and start swearing the most horrible things at us. We walked away saying nothing. I tried to wipe the food off of my face, only to feel a clump of mashed potato hit me in the back of the head. Sometimes it is hard being a missionary because right then I wanted to go back, grab that little man, and say, "EXCUSE ME!" But I didn't'" (Jeffrey R. Holland, "The Cost—and Blessings—of Discipleship," *Ensign,* May 2014, 6).

Elder Holland goes on to point out that these Sister missionaries were in the distinguished company of others who, though persecuted, have followed the Savior's example by reacting to evil treatment with kindness. Enduring ill treatment is sometimes the cost of discipleship; but enduring it without retaliation is always the hallmark of a disciple. In the case cited, the kind thing was to avoid retaliation and simply walk away. In other cases, a smile or sincere "Have a nice day" is about all we can do. But often, especially in ongoing relationships, there are many things we can do to treat those who mistreat us kindly. For instance, companions can look for opportunities to sincerely complement one another, both in private and before others. Shoes can be shined, chores done for each other, food shared, and weary hearts lifted. Companions can listen to and care about each other, even when they don't get the best treatment in return. Forgiveness, of course, must include heart, mind and action; but simply acting in a forgiving way can move one toward also thinking in forgiving terms, and having a forgiving heart.

Decide that whatever offends us really doesn't matter. The Sister missionary with mashed potatoes in her hair may remember the incident for the rest of her life. It's a great missionary story to share with family and friends. The anger she must have felt momentarily, however, is long gone. Other than as an interesting experience, the incident will not matter to her in the long term;

which is true of almost all incidents in which we are offended. Often we don't remember the subject very long after even an intense argument. Offenses don't matter over the long term, unless we do something in response that will have lasting consequences.

This being true, it makes sense to remember this fact in real time. Sister Rawlings was indeed offended by the gossip about her spread by a former companion. The problem made no real difference in her life as a missionary, however; and it became a total non-factor after her release from missionary service. It was much easier to forgive the offense when she reminded herself of this fact. When offended, it can help to ask our self, will I care about this 5 years from now, or even 5 months from now? Will this affect my eternal future? Is it really as bad as it feels?

It's Also Necessary to Forgive Ourselves

As a final thought on the importance of the principle of forgiveness in missionary service, the need to forgive oneself needs to be mentioned. The Lord makes no exception when He declares, "I, the Lord, will forgive whom I will forgive, but of you it is required to forgive *all* men" (D&C 64:10; emphasis added). We apparently need to include ourselves on the list of those we must forgive.

Elder D. Chad Richardson shared an interesting story about forgiving oneself involving W. W. Phelps, the author of the hymn "Praise to the Man", among others. At one point, Brother Phelps was one of those who attacked both the Church and the prophet Joseph. Along with other apostates, W. W. Phelps was involved in an affidavit against the Prophet issued in Richmond, Missouri, in November 1838. This affidavit was a part of the reason Missouri

Governor Lilburn W. Boggs's issued an extermination order against the saints. This resulted in their being driven from Missouri, while the Prophet and his associates were imprisoned for months in the dungeon of Liberty Jail.

As Elder Richardson points out, by 1840, Brother Phelps had a change of heart and plead for forgiveness, which was freely offered by Joseph Smith. Brother Phelps then penned the words to the hymn "Praise to the Man" which includes the words, "traitors and tyrants now fight him in vain". Quoting Elder Richardson, "How, I wondered, could Brother Phelps speak of traitors and tyrants fighting the Prophet when he himself had been one? Immediately I realized not only that Brother Phelps was no longer a traitor but also that he must have come to no longer see himself as one. The genuine, complete love and trust he received from Brother Joseph helped make it possible for him not only to forgive himself but also to erase his image of himself as a traitor" (D. Chad Richardson, "Forgiving Oneself", *Ensign*, March, 2007). This is a great story of forgiveness on the part of the Prophet Joseph; but also a good example of forgiving oneself, as Brother Phelps was apparently able to do.

As good as they are, missionaries are not perfect and they will make mistakes. When that happens, of course, they need to repent. But once done, it is then a requirement to forgive themselves and move on. To do otherwise is to deny the atonement. Ironically, some missionaries who believe strongly in the atonement and are quite effective in showing others how it can be applied, are not so good at applying it in their own life. Repentance is not complete and won't produce the emotional blessing it is designed to produce unless as part of that process, we forgive others *and also ourselves.*

In this regard, President Hunter taught, "It has always struck me as being sad that those among us who would not think of reprimanding our neighbor, much less a total stranger, for mistakes that have been made or weaknesses that might be evident, will nevertheless be cruel and unforgiving to themselves. When the scriptures say to judge righteously, that means with fairness and compassion and charity. That's how we must judge ourselves. We need to be patient and forgiving of ourselves, just as we must be patient and forgiving of others" *The Teachings of Howard W. Hunter,* ed. Clyde J. Williams, Deseret Book (1997), 34).

Of course, the need to forgive ourselves comes after we have done our best to repent of something, not before. The next chapter discusses the importance of commitment and self-discipline in missionary service.

CHAPTER TEN

MISTAKE TEN: NOT BEING SUFFICIENTLY SELF-DISCIPLINED

As discussed in previous chapters, some missionaries push themselves too hard and need to dial back a little. Other missionaries are half-hearted in their commitment and need to step up their effort. Since commitment levels tend to wax and wane over time, most missionaries will benefit from doing both at one time or another during their mission. Likewise, some missionaries will be doing fine in one aspect of their service; but will need to step it up, or cut back a little in another.

No matter the degree or extent of their commitment at the moment, all missionaries are likely to understand how important complete dedication is to a successful mission. This understanding may come from reading Section 4 of the Doctrine and Covenants, "see that ye serve him with all your heart, might, mind and strength, that ye may stand blameless before God at the last day" (D&C 4:2). Or it will have been made clear in their missionary preparation training, their MTC experience, and in instruction they receive during District and Zone meetings while serving. This truth is hard for a missionary to miss; yet not always easy to apply. This chapter is intended to provide suggestions on how to develop the self-discipline required to actually give the kind of dedicated service required. But first, let me expand on the normal definition of the term self-discipline.

Defining Self-discipline

The term self-discipline is synonymous with the terms self-control, self-mastery and will power. Most of us understand that all of these terms refer to the process of developing control over our thoughts and behavior; usually in the sense of ignoring body desires and natural tendencies in order to achieve some goal. All of these terms connote self-sacrifice, self-denial, and usually involve punishment and guilt when we fall short. More than the others, however, because of the similarity in spelling, the word self-discipline brings to mind the word disciple (discipline/disciple).

If we are a true disciple we are motivated to follow a cause by both faith and desire. The process of controlling ourselves can then be a positive and uplifting experience. It's not so much a matter of denying ourselves through punishment and sacrifice; but rather, more a matter of personal choice and an exercise in free will. We are obedient because we truly want to be, not because we think we have to be for some reason. When this is the case, doing the hard things to further a cause won't feel like we are repressing ourselves or grinding down our individuality. Rather it will be an emancipating and fulfilling experience.

The goal of every missionary and member of the Church of Jesus Christ of Latter-day Saints is to become a true disciple of Jesus Christ. Our goal is to consistently choose to think and act as He would. Attaining self-discipline in this sense means that we have faith that following the Savior is the best path; and it is a path that we are freely committed to follow. We may not understand or fully agree with some of the things our discipleship requires of us; and some of those things will require a degree of self-sacrifice; but our commitment is certain. Come what may, this is the horse we are determined to ride to the finish of the race.

Having settled this in our mind, we have done what the Savior asked us to do when he said, "…settle this in your hearts, that ye will do the things which I shall teach, and command you" (JST Luke 14:28). This in an important goal of all missionaries and members; because as Elder Neal Maxwell taught, settling this issue in our minds and hearts is a necessary precursor to consecration. Otherwise even missionaries may be no more than, quoting Elder Maxwell, "… 'honorable' members who are skimming over the surface instead of deepening their discipleship and who are casually engaged rather than anxiously engaged (D&C 76:75; D&C 58:27). Though nominal in their participation, their reservations and hesitations inevitably show through. They may even pass through our holy temples, but, alas, they do not let the holy temples pass through them" (Neal A. Maxwell, "Settle This in Your Hearts", *Ensign*, November 1992). In the same address, Elder Maxwell went on to point out the sometimes painful truth that those who shrink from deeper consecration are not worthy of Him who refused to shrink in his deepening agony during the Atonement (D&C 19:18).

Of course, becoming a fully consecrated disciple of Christ is a life-long pursuit for all of us. The fact that the great majority of us are not yet completely there is not nearly as important as is our commitment to the goal. In the meantime, how often do we think of doing something that would be good for us, but procrastinate, or simply don't do it? Or, conversely, how often do we recognize the damage inherent in particular behaviors but persist in them anyway?

Missionaries are no exception when it comes to this challenge. Whether it's a night person who is struggling to consistently get up on time, a missionary with obsessive thoughts that need to be managed, or someone who simply too often takes the easy way out; the need for self-discipline is obvious. Sister Baxter is a case in point. Among her several failings, she often sleeps in rather than getting up on time. She spends much of her study time daydreaming about home, relationships with other missionaries, and other non-mission related subjects. She loves to flirt with Elders and other young men; and she has developed a crush on a particular Elder who she has called a few times just to talk. She rarely takes the initiative in finding or teaching opportunities and she will do everything she can to extend visits with members beyond anything productive. Following are some ideas that might help Sister Baxter, or others with insufficient self-discipline.

Ideas That Can Help Develop Self-discipline

It will help to get her heart right. For one thing, as suggested above, Sister Baxter would benefit from settling in her mind the need to be a disciple of Christ. Would the Savior sleep in consistently? Would he be nonchalant about following mission rules and assignments? Would he spend so much time thinking about worldly things; and seeking social acceptance from the opposite sex and others? Sister Baxter needs to focus on reading the scriptures and prayerfully considering the absolute commitment Christ demonstrated in Gethsemane and on the cross;

and throughout His life. Doing so will inevitably build love and respect for the Savior; which in turn will naturally motivate her to be more committed in His service.

It would also help if Sister Baxter understood what she is missing by not being more committed. Again, prayerful consideration of scripture is a good place to start in coming to this understanding. One can't read very far in scripture without seeing examples of and/or hearing promises of inconceivable blessings to those who are obedient; and serious problems for those who are not. There are so many, but two of my personal favorites in this regard are Sections 84 and 88 in the Doctrine and Covenants. It's hard to contemplate the truths taught in these two sections of scripture without catching a vision of what's at stake in this life.

It is necessary to accept responsibility for her actions. Since we are talking about *self*-discipline, getting with the program will require Sister Baxter to do some things differently herself, on her own initiative. God can't answer her prayers if she doesn't pray consistently and sincerely. No matter how prayerful she is, she won't be inspired while acting in disobedience to mission rules. She won't be able to feel spiritual motivation and direction while her thoughts are on worldly things. This is true because God simply won't overrule her agency. Nor can He remove the inevitable consequences of the choices she makes; unless she repents that is, and qualifies for redemption through the atonement.

As we read in the Doctrine and Covenants, "There is a law, irrevocably decreed in heaven before the foundations of this world, upon which all blessings are predicated. And when we obtain any blessing from God, it is by obedience to that law upon which it is predicated" (D&C 130:20-21). We will never become a disciple of Christ by simply wishing it. It's not something that can be given to us, or even something we do. It's something we *become* as a result of consistently thinking and acting like He does. There is no short cut. "There is a law irrevocably decreed."

And should Sister Baxter or anyone believe that the requirements for discipleship are too hard, or even impossible to accomplish in their case, it's important to remember a truth taught in all four of our standard works. Quoting from the New Testament, "There hath no temptation taken you but such as is common to man; but God is faithful, who will not suffer you to be tempted above that ye are able; but will with the temptation also make a way to escape that ye may be able to bear it" (1 Corinthians 10:13). It may be hard, but it is possible; and those who approach the goal sincerely will have the help they need. As we read in Psalms, "God is our refuge and strength, a very present help in trouble" (Psalms 46:1).

It helps to remember in real time that I "want to" do this, not I "have to" to do this. As indicated above, a true disciple naturally wants to be obedient; but that is not always what he or she thinks at the point of choice. As her alarm went off in the morning, Sister Baxter would typically think, "Oh no, I have to get up. I'm so tired. I need my rest. I'll just relax here for a bit." An hour or two later she would finally get up. Obviously, she didn't have to get up on time; and thinking that she did was not very motivating. Sister Baxter would have been much more likely to get up on time if she had thought, "I'm so tired, but I want to get up. I want to be obedient. I want to get on with my day". We sometimes focus on the action and not so much on the thought underlying the action. It can help our motivation significantly when we monitor our thoughts in any given situation and choose to make them conform to our goal.

As a related point, it also helps to jump into a task before we are fully motivated to do it. Along with thinking, "I want to get up"; it would serve Sister Baxter well if she jumped out of bed before thinking about it too much at all. It would help even if she jumped out of bed provisionally, with the option of returning to bed later. I call this the ten minute rule. When faced with a task that we are not very motivated to do, it can help to at least get started. Motivation to continue and inspiration regarding how to proceed is much more likely if we at least start. For example, if Sister Baxter jumped out of bed, made her bed, and proceeded to get on with her day, it's very likely that she would stay up. Conversely, it's obvious what would happen if she waited in bed until she was motivated to get up.

It helps to do everything we can to protect ourselves against temptation. The Savior taught, "And if thy hand offend thee, cut it off; it is better for thee to enter into life maimed, than having two hands to go into hell, into the fire that never shall be quenched. And if thy foot offend thee, cut it off; it is better for thee to enter halt into life, than having two feet to be cast into hell, into the fire that never shall be quenched. And if thine eye offend thee, pluck it out; it is better for thee to enter into the kingdom of God with one eye, than having two eyes to be cast into hell fire" (Mark 9:43-44, 47).

Among other interpretations, it seems that these verses suggest the benefit in removing from our life those things that are contributing to bad choices. Sister Baxter, for example, loves to flirt and she has been breaking mission rules by telephoning another Elder just to talk. Flirting behavior has become a routine part of the way she relieves stress, builds her self-confidence, and it has become part of her personality. Her involvement with a particular Elder also brings a great deal of comfort and enjoyment. In essence, this behavior has become a part of her; like a hand, foot, or eye. It would be painful to give any of this up; similar to losing an appendage. As the Lord pointed out, however, the loss would be worth it if it meant avoiding something much worse.

To become a better disciple, Sister Baxter needs to be willing to cut off these enjoyable aspects of her life. She, of course, needs to be more than just willing. She must actually make the required change. This process could begin by giving up little things that contribute to the bigger problem. For instance, she might give the cell phone to her companion—especially at night when she was tempted to call the Elder. She might focus more of her time in missionary gatherings on the other Sister missionaries and not the Elders. She could ask her companion for help in noticing when she was flirting. This had become such a natural thing to do, she often wasn't even aware that she was doing it. Along with doing her part, she could ask the Elder friend to help her by avoiding contact during the remainder of their service. Finally, and most importantly, she could confess the problem to her Mission President and seek his help; which might include a transfer to a situation involving less temptation.

Setting goals is important; but it's even more important to promise to keep them. We often set goals that we don't achieve; and perhaps subconsciously never really expected to accomplish.

Reneging on a goal is often passed off as something to be expected. "Who among us always achieves our goals anyway?" Reneging on a promise is different. It's embarrassing to most of us; and we recognize that it says something about our character. In this respect, most of us would agree with Karl G. Maeser's definition of honor. "I have been asked what I mean by 'word of honor'. I will tell you. Place me behind prison walls—walls of stone ever so high, ever so thick, reaching ever so far into the ground—there is a possibility that in some way or another I might be able to escape; but stand me on the floor and draw a chalk line around me and have me give my word of honor never to cross it. Can I get out of that circle? No, never! I'd die first" (James E. Talmage, "Parables of James E. Talmage", *Deseret Book,* 1973).

Self-improvement goals are essentially promises; and it might help to think of them as such. I know a Sister missionary who found this to be true with respect to a goal to exercise more. She was much more consistent when she made a specific promise to herself and to her companion. She also gave a brief talk on the importance of following the missionary exercise schedule in a District Meeting, where she also publicly declared her intention. The pressure she felt to keep her promise helped keep her motivated to reach her goal.

Becoming self-disciplined requires spiritual help. Since difficult self-discipline goals require spiritual help, it's comforting to know that the needed help is always available. Any number of scriptures confirm this fact; including the Savior's promise found in the Doctrine and Covenants: "I will go before your face. I will be on your right hand and on your left, and my Spirit shall be in

your hearts, and mine angels round about you, to bear you up"
(D&C 84:88).

But of course, spiritual power requires that we sacrifice
pride. It requires us to accept responsibility for our problems, and
admit our need for help. It also requires that we put effort into
doing our part to keep the commandments. Sister Baxter had a
hard time admitting that she had a problem; and her thoughts and
actions were feeding and reinforcing the worldly side of her nature.
There were half-hearted attempts; but she was not praying,
studying, and serving in a way that would adequately feed the
spiritual side of her nature. No wonder the worldly side was so
much stronger and tended to dominate her spirit at this time in her
life.

Self-discipline with Love and Values, Not Fear and Guilt

Expanding on the theme of what it means to be self-
disciplined introduced earlier, some think that discipline has merit
as a standalone virtue. They see value in discipline simply for
discipline's sake, and they emphasize fear and guilt in their self-
mastery efforts. This is not a good idea according to President
Gordon B. Hinckley, who said, "Discipline imposed for the sake of
discipline is repressive. It is not in the spirit of the gospel of Jesus
Christ. It is usually enforced by fear, and its results are negative.
But that which is positive, which comes of personal conviction,
builds and lifts and strengthens in a marvelous manner. In matters
of religion, when a man is motivated by great and powerful
convictions of truth, then he disciplines himself, not because of
demands made upon him by the Church but because of the
knowledge within his heart that God lives; that he is a child of God

with an eternal and limitless potential; that there is joy in service and satisfaction in laboring in a great cause" ('The True Strength of the Church', *Ensign*, July 1973, p.48).

The discussion in Chapter Seven regarding managing through priesthood principles is also relevant here. There, a case was made regarding how ineffective and counter-productive it is when we exercise manipulation and control over our self or others. When we do things primarily out of guilt and fear, negative consequences are likely. Listing just a few of these:

1. When we try to force our self to do something we should, or avoid doing something we should not; the pressure must be sustained. We tend to rebel, and we will stop what we are forced to do when the threat is absent. If we put great pressure on ourselves regarding some point, it's impossible to keep that pressure on over the long term, and we will likely go back to the forbidden activity when we temporarily stop yelling at ourselves. Self-discipline works long term only if it is based in values and love. As President Hinckley suggests, when we do things because of our heartfelt belief, or out of love, motivation is natural and does not have to be artificially maintained.

2. Yelling at ourselves and emphasizing how bad our behavior is creates unhealthy stress. When we are overly self-critical, the emotional upset and stress created increases the need to experience something positive; the most direct temporary source of which might be entertaining a sexual thought or activity, sleeping in, or spending too much time with favorite Church members. In other words, putting too much negative pressure on ourselves can actually build the need to do the thing that we are yelling at

ourselves to avoid. It can even encourage a sense of entitlement. "I hurt so much, that I need to do this. It's the only way I can feel better."

3. Telling ourselves how horrible something we have done is, and focusing on how we must never do it again, sounds motivating; and it is, but only for the moment. It also reduces our self-confidence, or our faith in our self. It's important to build that faith, not tear it down. When tempted, it's much better to briefly review in our minds why we don't want to do whatever it is, and the advantages of exercising self-control, followed by putting our minds on to something else altogether—distracting our self as described earlier.

4. Fear and guilt encourage the creation of absolute and extreme goals; which are not likely to be met, resulting in a sense of failure and the tendency to give up. Using fear and guilt as motivators also encourages denying one's self of pleasure. Pleasure isn't evil. If defined as a fullness of joy, it's actually one of our ultimate goals (D&C 93:33). As explained below, self-discipline works best if it doesn't equate to self-denial.

As a side note, given the above points, there may be a question about why fear is sometimes used in scripture as a motivator. For instance, Enos in the Book of Mormon said of his people, "there was nothing save it was exceeding harshness, preaching and prophesying of wars, and contentions, and destructions, and continually reminding them of death, and the duration of eternity and the judgments and the power of God, and all these—stirring them up continually to keep them in the fear of the Lord" (Enos 1:23). Perhaps the truth is that fear is an attention getter and a basic motivator; and the only motivator effective in the case of those who have closed their heart to love and correct values. Sooner or later, however, if we are to be motivated to do disciplined things over time, our motivation must evolve into love for others, love for the truth, and heartfelt commitment to doing the right thing. As was pointed out earlier, that is clearly what motivates the Savior and our Heavenly Father.

Effective Self-discipline is Not Self-denial

Effective self-discipline is the opposite of self-indulgence; but it's also something quite different from self-denial. The scriptures warn us repeatedly about the negative consequences of self-indulgence; but self-denial is also a problem. As the prophet Nephi so famously said, "Adam fell that men might be; and men are, that they might have joy (2 Nephi 2:25). From scripture, we know that a fullness of joy requires both a body and spirit united together (D&C 138:17). This is true even to the point that those who have experienced a body, but who are temporarily without it as they await resurrection, will feel a substantial loss (D&C 45:17). In other words, bodies are a good thing, but they need to be managed effectively. And that's not easy for first time users like us. We have not had a body before and it takes some getting used to, and trial and error as we learn how to manage it properly.

To repeat the point; our bodies are good, even necessary if we are to experience a fullness of joy. We aren't designed to be robots. The body's appetites and passions have great value and need to be expressed; but only in healthy ways—only in ways that will do no harm to our self and others. The fact is, however, that because of our limited experience and vision, it isn't always clear what that means practically. Therefore, God has given us the boundaries. His commandments, as outlined in scripture, describe the bounds within which it is safe to function. There are unique rules that apply to missionaries which go beyond the normal boundaries described in scripture; but they are also given as a protection against choices that will damage the individual missionary or others.

When temptation arises to do something we know is beyond these boundaries, it helps to try to determine what we really want. "What is my basic motivation right now?" "What would feel good right now?" Of course, whatever we are tempted to do would feel good right now, but there are bound to be legitimate outlets for the same desire. For example, you may be hurting and just want to feel good for a minute. Laughing with a companion, relating positively to investigators and members, doing something nice for someone, reflecting on or anticipating some positive experience, and any number of other things could also be pleasurable.

It will take effort, a little ingenuity, and probably inspiration to discover legitimate alternatives for our compelling desires, but they are always there. Looking for and then doing these positive things is a much better strategy than just gritting our teeth and trying to stop the incessant desire that is about to overpower us. Doing the latter pretty much guarantees that we will be overcome; it's just a matter of time. On the other hand, meeting our needs through legitimate outlets largely removes the temptation; or at least, makes it much more manageable.

While working with missionaries in Europe and the Pacific Area, I saw how this works. Our young missionaries are wonderful. It's amazing the amount of self-discipline they have—totally not what would be expected from a typical population in their late teens and early twenties. They are human, however, and often quite young humans at that. Many have their issues, some involving a lack of self-discipline. I found that those with self-discipline problems generally went through cycles. When they were committed to the work, going the extra mile, and having success, they reported being relatively free of temptation. When they opted out temporarily, and were not following the program, their temptations became overpowering.

It's likely that they were less tempted at times, in part, because their positive actions built faith and commitment; meaning that their heart and mind were in the right place. But it's also true that when they were busy and doing what they should, their basic needs were met. They felt successful and productive. Through their service, they developed a motivating love for those they worked with, and for the Lord, which love is the greatest motivator of all. Their service also resulted in appreciation and love from those they served, which is also highly motivating. They felt hopeful and strong. They found excitement and interest in their work. Temptation was not a factor when these basic needs were met.

Self-discipline is Not an Inborn Characteristic.

Another general misconception about self-discipline is to think of it as an inborn characteristic, a lot like intelligence, which can't be altered that much. With this way of thinking, certain people are strong and others are weak-willed by nature. This leads some to think, "I just don't have enough will-power". This expression is sometimes used in a way that is intended to excuse a lack of self-discipline.

We all have our cross to bear, but the instruction remains the same. We may be tempted more than others in some aspect of our lives; but as the Lord said on a number of occasions, it's still required that we "Take up the cross and follow me" (Mark 10:21). And as clarified in the Joseph Smith Translation, "And now for a man to take up his cross, is to deny himself of all ungodliness, and every worldly lust, and keep my commandments (JST, Matthew 16:25-26). The prophet Alma also made a similar point to his son Corianton. "Now my son, I would that ye should repent and forsake your sins, and go no more after the lusts of your eyes, but cross yourself in all these things; for except ye do this ye can in nowise inherit the kingdom of God. Oh, remember, and take it upon you, and cross yourself in these things" (Alma 39:9). We are apparently expected to resolve whatever issues are holding us back; and a just God would not require something that is impossible. We can expect help if the task is beyond our ability.

Following the logic here, self-discipline is a skill that can be developed, not an inborn trait. It's a characteristic that all of us can develop to a greater degree. That being the case, like any similar trait, it can be developed through practice and repeated effort. Someone who has so far failed to reach a self-discipline goal has simply not yet been successful. The fact doesn't mean that they can't be successful, and it doesn't mean that they won't. As a matter of fact, everything in scripture promises us that we absolutely can do anything and everything that the Lord requests of us.

The Devil Didn't Make Me Do It!

Along with thinking "it's just the way I am", some excuse themselves by blaming Lucifer for their problems. Most missionaries are aware that the devil doesn't have the power to compel us to do anything; but some might still fall prey to thinking that their temptations are overwhelming. That thinking, in effect, means that Satan is at least indirectly controlling the missionary. Along with the scripture quoted earlier in this chapter which promises that we will never be tempted beyond our ability to resist (1 Corinthians 10:13), the following comments made by Joseph Smith are instructive. He was speaking about a notion, somewhat prevalent at the time, that Satan can control us.

> "Satan was generally blamed for the evils which we did, but if he was the cause of all our wickedness, men could not be condemned. The devil could not compel mankind to do evil; all was voluntary. Those who resisted the Spirit of God, would be liable to be led into temptation, and then the association of heaven would be withdrawn from those who refused to be made partakers of such great glory. God would not exert any compulsory means, and the devil could not; and such ideas as were entertained on these subjects by many were absurd." (Joseph Fielding Smith and Joseph Smith, *Teachings of the Prophet Joseph Smith*, Deseret Book, 1938, 187.)

There seems to be no escaping the fact that we have the power to withstand whatever temptation besets us. As we go about exercising that power, perhaps some of the suggestions given in this chapter will be helpful.

When Mental Health Problems are Overwhelming

As suggested, self-discipline is a skill we can develop; and Satan does not have the power to make us do things against our will. Some forms of mental illness, however, can overwhelm our agency. The power to manage our thoughts and actions is a universal gift; but it depends on a brain that is working normally. Some missionaries will find that their best efforts at self-discipline fall short; and even divine help does not seem to make the difference. In those cases, it is necessary that missionaries return home for treatment. Medication, therapy, and other treatment programs may be necessary. It's also sadly true that, in some cases, mental illness is beyond our current ability to treat effectively, even given the best medical help. When this is the case, resolution will need to wait on future blessings.

When mental health problems arise in missionaries, it becomes a major challenge for everyone concerned. The next chapter discusses factors associated with early release for mental health reasons; and how to minimize the trauma involved to the extent possible.

CHAPTER ELEVEN

THOUGHTS ON EARLY RETURNING MISSIONARIES

As indicated in the Introduction to this book, most missionaries handle the challenge of full-time missionary service with only temporary and relatively insignificant problems. Also, as indicated earlier, the Church provides a number of mental health treatment options to help those who have more serious issues. There still remains, however, a percentage of missionaries who have mental health problems that require treatment at home. Attitudes are changing for the better; but historically, this is a group that has often been judged unfairly, adding unnecessarily to the inevitable trauma involved in these situations. In this Chapter, the process by which a decision is made to send a missionary home early is described; followed by suggestions regarding how the returned missionaries should think about their early return; and how family, friends, and ward members should react.

The Decision Process

Following is a description of the process involved when sending a missionary home early for mental health reasons. This process was followed during the time and in the area of our service. It may or may not reflect the current procedure; or the process in all cases and in all areas of the Church. Based on our experience, when it became apparent to a Mission President that a missionary was struggling, he assumed the responsibility to make every effort to help the Elder or Sister cope. All Mission Presidents accepted this responsibility with compassion and inspiration. Mission Presidents and their wives provided counsel. Blessings were given, and any changes in assignment that might help were prayerfully considered. Where appropriate, medical doctors were asked to examine the missionary and provide whatever short-term treatment was required. Also where appropriate, mental health professionals were asked for advice on how to handle the problem; and/or they were asked to provide short-term therapy. The Stake President at home, and the missionary's family were alerted in cases where their love and support was needed.

In our experience, whatever help the situation called for was provided. But when serious symptoms persisted over time, the Mission President began the process to get the missionary home for treatment. The timing of this decision generally was based on prayerful consideration and input from others; but understandably, this process was begun immediately when there was a threat of physical harm to the missionary or others. No Mission President wants to send a missionary home early; but the decision must sometimes be made in order to protect the safety and health of the struggling missionary; and to minimize the negative impact these kinds of problems have on companions, other missionaries, and the work of the mission.

The actual decision to send a missionary home early for mental health or other reasons was made by a General Authority at Church Headquarters in Salt Lake City, not by the Mission President. The decision was made after getting input from a number of sources, including the Stake President at home who would have priesthood responsibility for the returning missionary, and the missionary's parents. Medical personnel involved were asked to report on their findings and recommendations. General Authorities who serve as members of Area Presidencies, and who have responsibility for the missionary in question, were also involved in the case and made recommendations.

Through this process, the Mission President relied heavily on an Infield Representative, or IFR, who represented the Missionary Department. Infield Representatives are former mission presidents with extensive experience in all aspects of missionary service. Their job is to provide counsel to the Mission Presidents they serve; and to act as a liaison between the Mission President, the Missionary Department, other interested parties, and General Authorities. Their job is to make certain that all of the required information has been obtained; and they supervise the logistics of the return.

All of this obviously took time under normal circumstances, but a system was in place that expedited the process in cases where immediate action was required. The safety of all missionaries is obviously a priority; and every effort was made to insure their safety, including providing escorts by medical personnel on the trip home when warranted.

Having been a part of this process in our two assignments as Mental Health Advisors, my wife and I can attest to the fact that everything that can be done to help missionaries will be done. Parents sometimes hear nothing but positives in letters home from their missionary son or daughter, and are surprised to learn that there is a serious problem. They then may assume, incorrectly, that priesthood leaders are acting too quickly without doing what they should to solve the problem in the field. They may also generally disagree with the decision to send their son or daughter home early. This is particularly true when symptoms are largely relieved on return home; and/or when things look different in hind sight. Again however, in our experience, these decisions are always made very carefully and prayerfully. Parents, and the missionary involved, can rest assured that each case has been handled in a very personal way; and it has been handled in a way acceptable to the Lord.

Advice to the Early Returning Missionary

How a missionary thinks about an early release for mental health reasons largely determines how difficult the experience will be from an emotional standpoint. It is sometimes hard to avoid negative thinking when family or friends misunderstand the situation; but the agency we all enjoy allows us the opportunity to think what *we* choose to think; not what others think—even those very close to us. In almost all cases, the following is true of an early returning missionary; and he or she should do everything possible to think as follows:

1. I did not make the decision to return home early. I was officially and formally released after prayerful consideration by my priesthood leaders.
2. I wanted to serve a full-term mission; and I tried hard to make that happen. I had a unique spiritual experience and am grateful that I was able to serve, even if for a shorter time than expected.
3. I am a returned missionary in every sense of the word. If anyone ever asks if I served a mission, I can proudly answer yes; and there is no need to add that my time in

the field was cut short. (Of course, this attitude may not be appropriate for someone who was released from service in the MTC before reaching their designated mission; or for those just barely in service. Generally those in this category can still take comfort in the fact that they were willing to serve; and they did everything they could to make it work. They, of course, can also focus on resolving the issues that made serving so difficult; and later pursue an opportunity to return to service as a proselyting or service missionary.)

4. I will focus on what I learned and the good experiences I had while serving; not on what I might have experienced if I had stayed the full term.

5. I will think of my experience similarly to a soldier wounded in combat. He or she accepted the call to serve their country, prepared well, and did their best. They returned with honor, and often even with medals. This was true whether they were wounded on their first day in combat or on their hundredth.

6. There is no difference whether I returned for mental health or physical reasons. Returning home because of my problem is no different than returning to mend a broken leg.

7. My problems do not reflect a lack of faith or commitment on my part. Nor do they suggest that my prayers were in vain. The Lord heard my prayers and they will be answered as He sees fit; and in the time frame that He knows is best for me. In fact, this whole experience may be an answer to prayer in that it

brought attention to a problem that I might not have addressed adequately under other circumstances.

8. My focus now is on getting better. I'm not going to worry about returning to complete my service until I feel like myself again. At that point, I can seek advice and inspiration regarding whether to reapply to complete my assignment.

9. If after I recover, I find that completing a proselyting or service mission is not what the Lord wants for me, I can still get on with my life and serve faithfully. All promised blessings are available whether or not I return to my mission. How I react to this and my degree of faithfulness from now on, will determine who I become.

10. Even if I am feeling better now, I need to see any treatment plan through. I need to do everything within my power, including taking any prescribed medications, to resolve the issue once and for all as I seek to reach my full potential.

In addition to thinking correctly, there are other things that will likely reduce the trauma of coming home from a mission early. These include:

1. Check in with your Bishop and schedule an opportunity to give a few brief remarks to your Ward as soon as possible. If at all possible, this needs to happen on the first day back to Church in your Ward. If you are not up to it, the Bishop could do this for you; but if you can, it is generally best if you make the statement.

2. Essentially, the idea is to briefly explain in general terms why you are home early. This can help ward members be more understanding; and it can help avoid having to answer the same question over and over again. You might say something like, "I am home earlier than I had expected for health reasons; but I am confident that I can get the treatment I need and get on with my life. It's good to see you again; and I appreciate your love and concern. I want you to know…"--then go on to bear a brief testimony. If true, this would be a good time to express gratitude for the experiences you had on your mission and express your intent to continue to serve faithfully in the future.

3. Imagine ahead of time some of the less than sensitive comments that family and friends might make and have an answer prepared ahead of time. For example, some may ask when you are planning to return to complete your mission. You might answer, "Well that's in the hands of the Lord (or "we'll see how things go"; or "I just don't have an answer for that yet"). For now I'm just going to do the best I can to get better and get on with my life." Some well-meaning ward members may push for detail regarding what the problem is and what you intend to do about it. You might answer, "I'm not comfortable getting into the details, but hey, how have you been anyway? Are you still (whatever)?" In other words, give a general answer and change the subject. If someone suggests directly or indirectly that you just need to put on a smiley face, buck up, and deal with life, remind yourself that your faith and commitment

are not the problem. Forgive the person suggesting otherwise, and change the subject.

4. Some may push you to share feelings or talk about your situation when you are not comfortable doing so. You might respond, "Thanks for your concern, but I'm not in the mood to get into all of that right now"—then smile and change the subject. You can also direct conversation to positive aspects of your service; e.g., how beautiful the country was, how much you enjoyed the people, how crazy the food was, and so forth.

5. Go to the temple, attend your meetings, accept callings, study, pray, and do everything you can to keep your testimony alive and growing. You may be tempted to minimize your involvement in the Church; but following through with that temptation would be among the worst things you can do.

6. If you are uncomfortable attending Church or in other Church activities, accept the responsibility for how you feel and don't blame it on your situation or on others. If you are uncomfortable, remind yourself that you have the power to change your thinking and/or approach in a way that will, if persisted in over time, change how you feel.

7. Get the rest you need, and follow medical advice; but be as active as possible. Getting plenty of exercise will pay dividends, as will serving others, and generally being busy. Sitting around, immersing yourself in video games, movies, or other forms of entertainment, withdrawing socially, or even spending too much time

analyzing your feelings and situation will not be
helpful.

8. In the rare instance in which family or friends simply
    cannot accept the early return and distance themselves
    from you, the only option is to forgive them. Act as
    normally around them as possible, and wait on them to
    see the error of their ways. That's bound to happen
    sooner or later. In the meantime, get on with your life
    by focusing on the things you can control; and don't
    worry about things, such as the attitude of others, that
    you cannot control.

Advice for Family and Friends

If you are family or a close friend to someone who returns
early from a mission, you have an important role to play. How to
best fulfill that role, however, can be confusing. Since every
missionary and problem is different, it's not possible to establish a
blueprint that will work in every situation. Even what will help the
same missionary at one point in time might not be helpful at
another. This fact leads to the need for parents and friends to be
inspired in how they approach their early returning missionary.
Sometimes talking about feelings will be helpful and sometimes it
won't. Encouraging Church and other activities may be a good
idea in some cases; but it will backfire in others. Even the early
returned missionary will not always know what he or she needs at
any given point in time. Only the Lord knows; and thus, the need
for inspiration. Even so, there are guidelines that are generally
applicable. Among these guidelines are the following:

1. Do not blame a mental health problem on the
    missionary. Such problems do not indicate a lack of

faith or unworthiness; nor do they stem from a weakness of character.

2. In the process of following the first suggestion, avoid being critical of the person, although you can be critical of the person's behavior or thoughts. For instance, the early returning missionary may share a feeling that he or she has failed the Lord in some way. Rather than responding with "No. That's not true! You shouldn't think that way!" It would be better to say something like, "I understand why you might think that; but you should know that I don't see it that way at all. You showed great faith to go on your mission in the first place, and I know you did the best you could under the circumstances. I don't believe that when people get depressed (or whatever) it means that they have a weak character or insufficient faith."

3. Do not put pressure on the returned missionary to return to finish his or her mission. That is a decision that needs to be made later under inspiration. It may or may not be the best idea at all; but certainly it is not healthy to bring it up early on; especially in the form of an expectation or demand.

4. Don't get into the game of "they should never have sent you home". As indicated above, these decisions are made by caring individuals with priesthood keys who have prayerfully sought to understand what is best for this particular missionary. Complaining about the decision in these cases does no good and can be dangerously close to "speaking evil of the Lord's anointed".

5. Review the advice to early returning missionaries given above and determine to follow the same advice when you interact with your family and friends. In other words, it's usually not necessary to get into details; and you want to be as positive and confident as possible.

6. Be a good listener and a shoulder to cry on. Don't be too quick to offer advice on what should and should not be done. Lecturing will almost always backfire.

7. Use your insurance, family, and Church resources to insure that adequate treatment is available. The Church has an after-care committee that can help in getting treatment to early returned missionaries in some cases. Basic responsibility, however, falls to the family, or to the local Church unit when the family is unable or unwilling to assist.

8. Reserve pressure on the early returned missionary to do things differently, or general criticisms, to only when "moved upon by the Holy Ghost (D&C 121:43). As discussed in previous chapters, when so inspired, use "I" messages rather than "you" messages. Complaints will usually be best received if offered as "I have a problem, and I need your help"; not "you have a problem and you had better get it fixed."

Advice for Ward Members

General ward members also play an important role in determining the experience an early returning missionary will have. Following are guidelines that might help.

1. Don't assume that the missionary has returned because of disobedience, a lack of faith, or insufficient commitment. It's best not to be concerned at all about the reason for the early return.
2. Don't seek details about what happened from the missionary, his or her family, or other ward members.
3. Don't avoid the missionary because you don't know what to say, or for any other reason. All you need to do is smile and welcome him or her home.
4. Think about and treat the person as you would any other returned missionary. Don't let the length of their service matter.
5. Don't speculate about the situation or pass on gossip.
6. Don't offer unsolicited advice about how to handle the situation or make comments that draw attention to the early release.

In line with the above suggestions, it's usually best if ward members avoid asking the following kinds of questions; or making comments such as:

What happened? Why did you get sent home?

When do you expect to be able to go back and finish your mission?

I know what you are going through, I … (then go on to share a personal experience or story about someone else in a similar situation).

Just be strong and have faith. I know the Lord will bless you if you do.

I'm so sorry you couldn't finish your mission.

You look so sad. What is bothering you?

Again, the goal for general ward members is to treat an early returning missionary as you would one returning full-term; and avoid whatever might bring attention to the reasons for the early release. At the same time, please don't ignore the returning missionary. Even if you don't know the person well, you can always smile and offer a heartfelt thanks for their service and welcome home. If you do know the missionary well, there will be plenty to talk about regarding the positive aspects of their missionary service, what has happened in their absence, shared memories, and so forth.

It's Not Easy

Mental health problems are hard enough to deal with in their own right. They can be even more difficult when they interfere with missionary service; which can lead to unnecessary guilt and feelings of failure. Hopefully, missionaries will be able to avoid the ten common mistakes outlined in previous chapters that can trigger or aggravate mental health problems. When significant problems arise in spite of their effort and faith, the mental health resources available to serving missionaries will hopefully resolve the issue. When the problem continues in spite of all efforts, it is up to the missionary to accept the situation and deal with it in a healthy way, as suggested earlier. As also explained above, family, friends, and ward members can step up to help in ways that won't make the situation worse. In all such cases it will help to remember the Lord's promise, "He that is faithful in tribulation, the reward of the same is greater in the kingdom of heaven. Ye cannot behold with your natural eyes, for the present time, the design of your God concerning those things which shall come hereafter, and the glory which shall follow after much tribulation. For after much tribulation come the blessings" (D&C 58:2-4).

This wonderful insight and promise from our Savior certainly applies to missionaries who struggle with mental or physical problems that require an early release; but it applies equally to missionaries who return early for other reasons, including disobedience to gospel and mission rules. Repenting and having the courage to face problems head on, in spite of the shame and embarrassment that may be felt when the problem is of one's own making, can obviously be a huge test. I know personally those who have done this hard work and have emerged blessed and strong. Those who know the story, including of course the Lord, have great admiration for these individuals. The fact of their mistakes are forgotten and the strength manifested in their courageous repentance is respected. The fact of a life well lived is all that matters going forward.

But again, the best option when possible, is of course to resolve issues before or during one's missionary service in a way that avoids the necessity of an early release. The next chapter summarizes the ideas presented in earlier chapters that can help missionaries do so.

CHAPTER TWELVE

SUMMARY SUGGESTIONS TO SOLVE VARIOUS PROBLEMS

This chapter summarizes the suggestions made in previous chapters regarding how to handle various problems that may come up in missionary service. These suggestions are presented in outline form under the heading for specific issues. Summarizing the concepts in this way is intended to provide a short-cut reference that can be used by missionaries who are experiencing the issues discussed. It will hopefully also be of help to parents who have a missionary son or daughter troubled by one of these issues; and to others who are concerned about missionary welfare.

Specific topics followed by the page numbers where the summary is provided are as follows:

Anger and irritability Problems

238

1. *Pray for help in forgiving and distracting.* As mentioned earlier, you can't pray anger away if you continue to think in ways that sustain and grow your angry feelings. This, of course, is often easier said than done. Thankfully, divine help is available.

2. *Calm Down*

    a. Where possible, move away from the irritating situation, take time out. The part of your brain that creates an angry feeling is quicker to respond than the part of your brain that can reason and make good decisions. Find a way to give yourself time for the reasoning and good judgement to kick in.

    b. Take a deep breath, or a series of them. Tell yourself you are not going to let whatever you are concerned about matter.

    c. Count backwards, sing a hymn, and recite a favorite forgiveness scripture (i.e. D&C 64: 8-10); or distract your thinking by focusing on something other than the issue that is annoying you.

    d. Think peaceful thoughts. DO NOT review the problem in your mind.

3. *Rethink the situation.*

    a. Remember that in the longer term whatever you are mad about doesn't really matter! The only thing that matters is how you respond to the provocation.

    b. Consciously decide to let the other person get away with it and then think about something else. Don't dwell on the problem.

    c. Literally count your many blessings and think about the good things in your life.

d. Remember that the Lord requires us to manage our anger; and He does not require anything of us that is not possible. (1 Nephi 3:7)

e. Look for triggers of your anger and think of ways to avoid them.

f. Don't think about or try to handle frustrating things or people when you are hungry, angry, frustrated, stressed out or tired.

g. Try to think positively about people/situations that frustrate you. Yes there are obvious problems; but what is good about him/her, or the situation?

h. Avoid thinking in absolutes.

4. *Be willing to apologize, serve, and try to understand those who trigger your anger.*

a. Look in the mirror when you are angry. You may not like what you see.

b. Take the higher road by being willing to apologize. Genuinely ask for what you can do to make things right.

c. Follow the direction from the Lord to "do good to them that hate you, and pray for them who despitefully use you and persecute you" (3 Nephi 12:44).

5. *Keep an anger log.* For one week, record the "trigger events" that seem to spark your anger, what you were angry about, and how you handled the anger. Based on your findings, prayerfully develop a plan for how to handle the "trigger events" differently next time.

6. *Learn constructive ways of dealing with problems.*

a. Ask for what you want, but don't insist or demand.

b. Own the problem rather than blaming/attacking the other person. Find ways to solve the problem on your own where possible; and decide not to worry about it when that isn't possible.

c. Try to understand the other person. Ask specific questions to check your conclusions about the other person; e.g., "That comment makes it sound like you think I am an idiot. Is that what you really meant to say?"

d. As described in Chapter Three, use the magic words, "You might be right" when you disagree with someone; or when they disagree with you.

e. Work for a "win/win" solution when your opinions or wishes conflict with others. It's almost always possible to reach a compromise that works for everyone when all parties involved are sufficiently humble and forgiving. Of course, you can't guarantee that someone else will be humble and forgiving; but you can insure that you are.

Boredom--Feeling That You Are Wasting Your Time.

1. Break up the day so that you don't spend too long on any one activity. Intersperse activities that are particularly difficult or uncomfortable for you with activities that you enjoy.

2. Work hard for a time and then take a short break and just enjoy your companion and surroundings. Then go back to work. Remember that when out and about, even if not actively proselyting at the moment, you are still on duty and available for anyone the Lord might direct to you. If

you feel guilty about taking a break, remember that you can cut more wood if you take time out to sharpen the saw.

3. Make a goal to be yourself. Have fun with your companion. Share fun stories and uplifting experiences. Bring humor into the mix.

4. Prayerfully review and write down all of your reasons for deciding to serve a mission. Remember that the Lord values your service, even when there are no obvious positive outcomes from your work. This is true because:

   a. There may be a positive outcome that can't be seen.

   b. Being obedient and serving faithfully when results are meagre proves you are not a "fair weather" disciple.

   c. It's important to the Lord that everyone has an opportunity to accept the gospel, whether they actually accept the invitation or not.

   d. Any great accomplishment requires great sacrifice.

Companionship Problems

1. See this as an opportunity to become more forgiving; especially if your companion doesn't deserve your forgiveness and/or keeps offending you even though you have asked for cooperation.

2. Don't try to fix your companion. Look for his or her strengths. Do nice things for him or her—whether the kind treatment is deserved or not.

3. Avoid swearing in the biblical sense; which means avoid making black and white statements about things. Use the magic words, "You might be right" in all instances where there is a difference of opinion.

4. Share your concerns briefly by concisely using an "I" message, not a "you" message: e.g., I have a problem and I would like your help with it; not you have a problem and you had better fix it.
5. Don't insist that things be fair or that justice be served. Forgive no matter what.
6. Remember that the situation is temporary. It makes an interesting chapter in your mission experience; but assuming you handle it well, it will have no impact on your future.

Crowded Feeling—Insufficient Alone Time

1. Reassure your companion that there is no problem; but ask for some quiet time to think.
2. Create a sense of privacy at times by writing, praying, reading, or planning.
3. When practical, take a little more time than normal in the bathroom; and do some deep breathing and brief meditating.
4. Focus on the positive aspects of the experience you are having; including the advantages of always being in the presence of a companion. It's not all bad.

Depressed Feelings

1. Start by not being overly concerned that you are depressed. Some level of depression is normal at one time or another. Worry about depression will often make it worse. At the same time, you want to do what you can to lighten your mood.

2. It usually helps to be busy. Too much time thinking about oneself is not healthy. Focus on others and what you can do for them; not on why you are depressed and how to get past it.

3. Listen for self-critical or generally negative thinking and redirect to unrelated and more positive topics. Insist on thinking more positive thoughts, even if your feelings remain negative.

4. Review the discussion regarding unrealistic expectations in Chapter One. Make certain that your expectations for your mission are reasonable.

5. Include potentially pleasurable activities in your schedule, even if at the moment you find no pleasure in them. Take a few more short breaks than normal; but work as hard as possible in between breaks. Look for things for which you are grateful. List at least three things for which you are grateful at the end of each day. Sing appropriate songs to yourself, look for the positive and humor in whatever happens. Include interaction with positive people and situations where possible.

6. Get a priesthood blessing and call on God's help to think and act positively, even if you don't feel positive.

7. If the depression persists in spite of your efforts to lighten the mood, advise your Mission President and follow through on whatever medical intervention he may suggest.

Discouragement—Working Hard but Not Reaching a Goal

1. Remember that great, dedicated missionaries have served successfully without having many, if any, converts. Aaron, when compared to Ammon at one point in the Book of

Mormon, is an example. President Hinckley is a good modern-day example.

2. Your success is defined by your obedience, effort, and attitude; all of which is within your control. It is not defined by the number of progressing investigators you have at the moment; which is not within your control.

3. With personal goals, look at your progress as being like walking along a board or rail, not climbing a ladder. You are not a "La**dd**er-day Saint"—meaning that if you slip up you fall to the bottom of the ladder and have to exert extreme effort just to get back to where you were; let alone make progress. It's hard to be motivated with that mindset. Working at goals should be thought of as more like walking along a narrow board or rail. You may fall off; but all the progress made before falling off counts. You then just need to get back on the rail and put maximum effort into staying on course going forward.

4. Have the goal to do the best you can *under the circumstances*, not the best you can under the best of circumstances. Who sets out to teach a bad lesson, or have a bad mission? That happens only when we lose faith/hope and quit trying. Often we can't change the circumstance that limits our ability (health, companion assigned, area assigned, and so forth); but the Lord can. He knows the impact the circumstance has on our performance; and if He is concerned about our situation, He will certainly change the circumstance. If we are doing our best, the Lord will be happy with our effort even if it falls short of our expectation.

5. You know that you are doing your best when you are committed and prayerful about reaching a goal; but you can't think of anything more you can do to accomplish it, other than what you have already been doing. At that point, you should continue your effort, and be open to new ideas; but you can rest assured that you are doing your best. Again, if the Lord wanted you to do more, or something different than your current effort, He would make that known to you.

6. Set reasonable, practical, obtainable goals; and give yourself credit for movement toward those goals. Focus on successes in reaching a goal, not failures.

Eating Problems

1. Eating in a healthy way can be a particularly difficult challenge in some cultures where overeating and/or not having the best diet is normal. In these cases, you can use an "I" message to ask for cooperation; e.g., "Thank you so much for offering (the second helping) but I have been having some stomach issues and, as much as I would like to, I just can't eat any more". In a similar way you can ask to be excused from eating anything that your system has trouble digesting. You still may get the sense that you are offending your hosts, or they may chide you for being too thin or too concerned about your weight. Even so, with a smile and relaxed attitude about it; usually there is no damage done.

2. Ask for your companion's cooperation in keeping fast foods and unhealthy snacks to a minimum. Again, use an "I" message, not a "you" message; i.e., I have a problem

and need your help; not you have a problem and need to change.

3. Work with your companion to develop a meal plan for the week before shopping. Make certain that healthy foods are included to the extent possible.

4. Avoid food fetishes or too much concern about how much you weigh and what your diet is doing to you. Often times, worry about what you are eating is worse on your body than a less than ideal diet. There will be plenty of time to lose weight or better manage your diet when you are back home and have better resources and more control over your environment.

5. Remember that when you look in the mirror there is an excellent chance that you see a heavier and less attractive person than others see. Common perceptual distortion makes that true for most of us.

6. Take healthy snacks with you and don't go too long before eating something.

7. If you have had an eating disorder in the past, or your eating concerns are extreme, talk to your Mission President. He may suggest professional help.

Fear and Panic

1. Learn to avoid excessive or unnecessary worry (see page 231). This can cut panic off at one of its primary sources.

2. Move your thinking from "have to" or "need to", to "want to". Anytime you need something to happen and it doesn't happen; or even if it just looks like it might not happen, you will get anxious. As an example, wanting to be on time and taking all steps practical to be on time is a good idea.

Needing to be on time will create unnecessary anxiety when circumstances come up that make you late in spite of your good intentions. Needing to stop the symptoms of a panic attack will make the symptoms worse. Don't try to talk yourself out of the feelings you have, or even minimize them. Just try hard not to focus on them.

3. When you first notice fear or panic, take several deep breaths and think calming thoughts. Practice deep breathing frequently over time in order to develop a "relaxation response". Deep breathing alone can curtail a building panic attack. It is most effective when coupled with thought control (see page 225).

4. When you first notice panic feelings building, label this as a panic attack. Your brain is releasing stress chemicals which are causing you to feel the way you do for no good reason. There is no danger. Then try very hard to move your thinking to something other than what your body is doing. Get into a conversation with someone, walk around, or do anything that will help you focus on something outside of yourself.

5. Pray hard; but not necessarily for the feeling to go away. Rather pray for help in distracting and knowing what to do to get your mind off of the horrible feelings you are having.

Getting Up on Time

1. Review the reasons that you want to get up on time. Make sure that your thoughts are "I want to get up"; not "I have to get up".

2. Jump out of bed without thinking about it, make your bed, and get into some form of exercise right away—muscle

248

stretching would be great. Give yourself permission to take a short power nap during the lunch hour if you need more sleep.

3. Turn on the lights, or if practical, get a timer that will turn a light on automatically about ten minutes before it is time to get up. Light signals the brain to wake up.

4. Have something in mind that will feel good after you arise; e.g., sharing something fun with your companion, having breakfast, or maybe just a quiet time to yourself.

Headaches and Stomach Problems

1. When headaches and digestive problems arise and persist to the point that they are making it difficult to do your work, you should let the Mission President know. It may be recommended that you see a physician.

2. Headaches and stomach problems are often signs of stress. To look at that possibility, you may want to keep a log for a week or two of when problems arise. Look for patterns that may help identify sources of stress. Then do what you can to reduce the stress.

3. There are many techniques available to help reduce stress. Among many others, these include identifying and changing thinking that causes unnecessary stress, deep breathing and relaxation exercises, taking more frequent breaks, and limiting personal goals to one at a time. This book and the *Adjusting to Missionary Life* booklet give detail on what can be done to better manage stress levels. You might also ask your Mission President about the possibility of consulting with an Area Mental Health Advisor, or other mental health professional.

Homesickness

1. Don't be overly concerned about the fact that you are homesick. It is natural, especially if being away from home is new for you. Most missionaries go through a period of homesickness at some point.
2. Keep reminding yourself that the homesick feelings are temporary. You will not always feel this way.
3. Get up and get busy. The very best way to combat homesickness is to distract yourself from worry or self-pity. Being involved and keeping busy can be a great distraction.
4. Follow the guidelines in Adjusting to Missionary Life (pages 29-30). These include, unpacking and settling in; reviewing your reasons for coming on a mission, seeking a priesthood blessing, removing distracting reminders of home, and being patient. It may take time; but the feelings will change.

Insomnia

Sleep Hygiene Principles

1. Use the bed for sleeping only – no reading, study, problem solving, or talking on the phone while in bed.
2. Each missionary should have a comfortable bed that fits his/her frame. Alert mission leaders if you need a better bed. There should also be a private and secure area created around your bed with familiar and comfortable objects such as a comfortable personal pillow, photos of family, religious pictures, etc.
3. Where possible, arrange for a comfortable temperature and noise barrier such as ear plugs. Ear plugs come in different

shapes and sizes and you may need to experiment to find a comfortable pair that work for you.

4. Use the last hour of the day to unwind and relax. Write in a journal (unless doing so gets you thinking too much about problems at home or in the mission), have a snack (avoid sugar), listen to appropriate music, talk to your companion, or do other calming activities.

5. Wake up at the same time each morning (including P-day) no matter how much sleep the night before. That means covers off, feet on the floor, and lights on full.

6. Do your best to eat right and exercise daily, but no heavy eating or exercise within an hour of going to bed.

7. Be careful to take medications as prescribed. Milk is good at night but obviously avoid any stimulants.

8. Don't worry about not getting enough sleep. Avoid pressuring yourself by thinking "I have to get to sleep". You are probably getting more sleep than you think you are and our bodies can adjust to periods of inadequate sleep. You may also be able to schedule a 15 to 20 minute power nap later in the day. (Longer naps are counterproductive and can exacerbate insomnia.)

9. If you can't seem to stop thinking about them, write down the things you are worried about, or things you need to do; then put the list away and tell yourself you will work on action plans in the morning.

10. Do your best to maintain a grateful, positive and optimistic view throughout each day--even on the tough days when things don't go all that well. Focus bedtime prayers on gratitude, not problems. Save more detailed prayers in which you seek help and solutions for the daytime.

The relaxation induction protocol that follows is a 4-step procedure designed to gradually move an individual into a physically and then mentally relaxed state. It should be followed religiously over a period of at least three weeks— even if it doesn't seem to be helping that much. In other words, don't just try it for a night or two and then give up if it doesn't seem to be helping.

STEP ONE: Get into bed at the same time each night after a familiar bedtime routine. Get as comfortable as possible and then let the thought pass through your mind, "This is my time to relax. I get eight hours off. I don't have to solve any problems, or deal with any worries until tomorrow." Consider briefly the following points: (1) Since the Lord knows you have a sleep problem, He won't bother you with inspiration during the night. This is your time off. (2) You want to get to sleep, but you don't NEED to. Your body and brain can at least relax. Feeling a need to fall asleep is a good way to stay awake. After considering these points, move through the next steps.

STEP TWO: Breathe in deeply using your stomach (diaphragm) to the count of four. Hold that air in for an additional count of four. Then let the air out through your lips slowly to the count of eight. This is called the 4-4-8 breathing technique. Do this for several minutes as you focus on settling into the bed, while noticing and relaxing any muscle tension in the shoulders, or anywhere in your body.

STEP THREE: Return to normal but deep and rhythmic breathing. The goal now is to put your mind onto something engaging that won't lead to thinking about problems. Some suggestions include: Think of all the blessings or good things in your life that begin with each letter of the alphabet. Or think of all the animals you can, the names of which begin with each letter of the alphabet. Count back from 100 in threes. Assume that money is no object and build your dream home in your mind. Where would the home be located? Design the grounds, the exterior and interior. Furnish it. What kind of electronics would it include? Or build a sailboat, in great detail, in your mind and then take it on a solo trip through the Pacific. Sing comforting songs in your head or say a silent prayer of thanksgiving. In short, engage your mind on any subject that doesn't lead to worry or concern.

STEP FOUR: If you are still awake after 20-30 minutes, get up, get some fresh air and then go back to bed and repeat steps 2 through 3. You can also go through these steps if you wake up in the night and have trouble falling back asleep. When that happens, realize that periods of light sleep are normal through the night and you might be sound asleep when you think you are awake. Rather than worry about being awake, just be grateful that you don't have to get up yet; and that you can enjoy the bed for at least a bit longer. Certainly, if you worry about being awake, the resulting stress increases the chance you will come fully awake.

As a final note, sleep problems often result from excessive stress in one's life. Use the Adjusting to Missionary Life Materials to help identify what those sources of stress might be, and follow the suggestions given. You can also speak with your Mission President or his wife about chronic problems. In those cases, you may be referred to the Area Mental Health Advisor.

Loving the People You Serve is Hard

1. Remember that love can be a verb. It can define what we do, not just what we feel. We love others by serving them. It's nice, but not necessary, to also have warm, feelings for them.
2. See the faults in others as a great opportunity to get better at forgiving.
3. Pray for the gift of charity and do everything you can to serve those around you.
4. Avoid thinking that any unloving feelings you have, or the absence of loving feelings for those you serve, makes you unworthy to be a missionary. You want to change such feelings where possible (by changing your thinking); but don't let these kinds of thoughts get in the way of your mission responsibilities and service.

Masturbation and Pornography Temptations

1. Follow the guidelines where practical that you teach investigators regarding addiction recovery (Preach my Gospel (pages 188-190).
2. Implement the ideas under the heading Sexual Thoughts That are Oppressive (page 228).

3. Certainly work to overcome any problem in this area; but don't let guilt become overwhelming. Share the problem with your Mission President. If he agrees, understand that you can still work effectively as a missionary so long as you are diligent in your effort to overcome the problem; and are committed to ridding it from your life.

4. Invest fully in your missionary work. Don't let the problem keep you from serving with everything you have. Such service is often very helpful in overcoming temptation and relieving tension.

5. Make sure you are exercising and eating properly; and getting sufficient rest.

6. Call on the Lord for help of course; but also ask your Mission President for help; and perhaps a Mental Health Advisor if available.

Mission Leaders Are a Problem

1. Remember that your time under the direction of a difficult leader is temporary. Whatever is happening simply won't matter at some point in the near future.

2. Think of this as another opportunity to get good at forgiving; and learn from the experience. Learn to handle the frustration without letting it interfere with your work. Decide how you will do things differently when it's your turn to lead.

3. Remember the great value in developing the virtue of humility (D&C 112:10). Take counsel and ask for suggestions on how you can improve. Thank leaders for their service, even if you quarrel with their approach in some respects.

4. The bad stands out, but look for the good in your mission leaders. They are not perfect; but they all have redeeming qualities. They, like you, are a work in progress. None of us is done yet.

Obsessive Negative Thoughts:

1. Challenge negative thinking. When troubled about something, write down the thoughts you are having about the issue. Then rewrite each thought so that the new thought reflects the truth, but in a positive way. For example, you may write down that you are thinking, "I don't know the language well enough. I can't do this" A more correct and positive rewrite might be "I don't have to be great with the language to speak with the Spirit. I will just do the best I can and the Lord will make up the rest".

2. Follow a simple ADD strategy; which stands for Awareness, Decision, and Distraction. When you are aware of an unwanted thought (A); decide (D) to not go there in your mind; and then distract (D) your thinking by focusing on something unrelated to the unwanted thought. Repeat these steps as many times as it takes until the obsessive thought goes away. This will often mean many repetitions at first; but you will get better at distracting with time.

3. Distract from unwanted thoughts in any number of ways. Talk to someone. Ask yourself or others intriguing questions. Sing hymns, quote scripture, prepare a lesson or talk. Go to neutral in your thinking by naming blessings that start with each letter of the alphabet; or remembering the names of animals that start with each letter of the

alphabet. Imagine in detail a safe, happy place and go there in your mind.
4. Follow the guidelines for controlling excessive worry (see page 231).

Procrastination

1. Follow the "ten-minute rule". Establish a rule with yourself that when it's time to do a project, you will spend at least ten minutes on it even if you aren't in the mood; even if you don't have the time to complete it; and even if you don't know how to proceed. Motivation and inspiration on how to proceed often come after starting a task. Don't wait for the motivation and inspiration to come first.
2. Break big tasks down into little ones. Instead of trying to do all of a complicated task at once, it helps to break it down into manageable bites with a timetable and plan on when to complete each piece.
3. Avoid thinking that whatever you do has to be perfect. Something is usually better than nothing. Waiting until you can do something perfectly is a common cause of procrastination.
4. If you get the thought, "I really don't want to do this", remind yourself that once a decision has been made that completing an assignment is important for some reason, the fact of not wanting to do it is irrelevant. All this means is that you had better start the project so that you can get it over with as soon as possible.

5. Delegate and get other people involved where possible. Things that are hard to do are usually easier if done with others.

6. Publically commit to doing whatever it is you would like to do. The probability goes up that you won't procrastinate if you have made a public commitment.

Self-confidence is Low

1. Review Doctrine and Covenants 121:45. Charity and virtuous thought are the two ingredients mentioned if you are to have "confidence before the Lord." Letting charity "fill our bowels" means to have charity, deep inside. It means to be patient, long-suffering, and kind toward yourself as well as others. Any critical and negative thoughts you have about yourself are definitely uncharitable, and will have an obvious negative impact on confidence. To let "virtue garnish our thoughts unceasingly" can mean more than to avoid unclean thought. Thoughts that are negative, pessimistic, and that bring you down can also be thought of as unvirtuous.

2. Make bite-size goals and then do things that are hard for you. For some that might be talking to strangers when out and about, making comments in Church classes and missionary meetings, or giving talks. Review Moses 6:31-32. The prophet Enoch was young and slow of speech when called. In spite of his handicap, the Lord asked him to open his mouth—to practice doing that which was hard for him. Over time, he became a great orator.

3. Review Moses, Chapter 1 in the Pearl of Great Price and other scriptures which identify who you really are. Once

Moses understood God's power, and most importantly, that he was a son of God, Moses was able to rebuke Satan and resist his temptations. Exactly like Moses, you are also a son or daughter of God with infinite potential. This is true in spite of whatever temporary problems or weaknesses you have. Understanding the infinite worth you have can boost confidence, even when others may not seem to see it.

4. Confidence goes down when you keep failing at something; which always happens if your goals are too high. Realize that you will sometimes be tempted to do too much of a good thing. Some missionaries are basically immune to temptation to do something overtly evil. But they may still be tempted to do too much of a good thing; which will also cause problems. Examples of this include missionaries who feel that their best isn't good enough; or those who accept higher standards for themselves than the Lord has established; e.g., fasting too often, or working more than the recommended number of hours.

5. Keep a sense of humor when you make a mistake. If you worry about making a mistake ahead to time, ask yourself what the worst thing is that might happen. Generally the worst thing that can happen will be something you know will not be the end of the world. It will be something you know you can handle with the help of the Lord.

6. Cheerfully do what you can and know that the Lord will make up the difference. What you do doesn't have to be perfect; nor does it need to be as good as others might be able to do.

Sexual Thoughts that are Obsessive

1. As long as they are unwelcome and you don't dwell on them, having unclean thoughts does not make you unclean. You will be judged by "your" thoughts—meaning those thoughts that you encourage, enjoy, expand upon, and relish. Desires can be generated by the pleasure centers in your brain, and Satan can suggest inappropriate things; but all of that is common temptation. In an important sense, thoughts coming from these sources are not "your" thoughts. These kinds of thoughts and desires make you unclean only if acted upon; or when you encourage them.

2. Intense guilt, getting upset with yourself for having such thoughts, and making the problem a really big deal makes it harder to distract from and control your thinking. It leads to a loss of confidence which makes self-control more difficult. Following the Savior's example, it's best to recognize unclean thought as temptation and then simply give it no heed (D&C 20:22). Distract yourself, and move on from temptation. Don't let it define you.

3. You will have the easiest time controlling sexual thoughts when you are busy and involved in the work. Ironically, some missionaries who have sexual thoughts feel so guilty, and become so upset by the fact, that they pull back from their service; which will make the temptation worse.

Social Problems--Not Feeling Respected and Appreciated by Others

1. Be a good listener. You don't have to be the life of the party to be enjoyed by others. Every performer needs an audience and you can be that audience.

2. Focus on being kind to others and enjoying their company, not worrying about what you are about to say or do. Self-conscious thought and concern leads to not participating adequately in social situations and/or odd behavior that calls attention to yourself in a negative way.
3. Try hard not to take things personally, to argue with others, or to engage in self-pity.
4. Share yourself with others and seek to learn more about them.
5. Be as positive and upbeat as possible in your demeanor (smile easily); and also in what you choose to think. Remember that what you think is often communicated nonverbally, even if you don't say it.

Social Problems—Difficulty Talking to Strangers.

1. Turn your attention to the needs of others rather than focusing on what you are feeling and thinking. Ask yourself, what is he or she thinking? What are they feeling right now? What is important to them?
2. As you see someone you would like to talk with, try to mentally communicate your interest (not in words). For example, think, "I really care about you", or "You are important to me". Doing this can establish a welcoming mindset. Along with these thoughts, smile and make eye contact.
3. Set reasonable goals to introduce yourself to one new person at each meeting you attend. Set goals to strike up conversation with a given number of strangers each day. This should be a number that stretches you, but is still doable.

4. Learn to make observations or ask questions that strike up conversation without being intrusive. Usually these are positive comments about something you observe, "Your kids are adorable", or "Your hair is stunning", or "You look happy this morning." If this is not natural, look at how others who are talented in this area do it. Ask others for their help and then practice—practice both in your mind and by role-playing.

5. Learn how to end conversations comfortably. Learn how to excuse yourself if the conversation stalls, if you notice the other person is not interested, or if you have discussed what you felt was important and the other person is not interested. Again, if this does not come naturally, you can learn by observing others and seeking their help.

Spiritual Disconnect—Not Feeling the Spirit or Prayers Don't Seem to be Heard

1. Don't automatically assume that the problem is your unworthiness. If there is some area where you know you are being disobedient, it obviously makes sense to repent; but there are other reasons you might not feel the Spirit.

2. Remember that missionaries will have the Spirit with them if they are committed and obedient; but they may not feel it. This is true if you are depressed, anxious, or distracted in any way.

3. Your prayers will be answered; but not necessarily in the manner or in the timeline you expect. God will bless you in all ways needed; but not necessarily in all ways desired. Prayers for things that are actually not in your best interest, and/or in the best interest of others, will not be answered.

4. Sometimes whatever you decide to do is fine with the Lord. Other times, it doesn't matter what you do, the outcome will be the same. In those cases inspiration may not be forthcoming. When this happens, it is often an indication of the Lord's confidence in you, not His disappointment.
5. Just keep doing the best you can to serve well. Good feelings and blessings will follow your best efforts; but perhaps not in the time frame you expect.

Worry that is Excessive

1. Take some time to list the things you have been worried about recently. Then go through the list and identify each worry as either (A) a worry that you practically can do nothing about; (B) a worry you can do something about; or (C) a worry you aren't sure whether you can do something about or not. First, work on all "A" worries. Whenever they come to mind, immediately focus on something unrelated. Don't try to talk yourself out of the worry, decide not to think about it at all. Keep refocusing as often as necessary in order to avoid thinking about the worry issue in any way. Next, make a plan and schedule a time to do whatever practical thing you can do about each "B" worry. Do what you can and then decide not to worry about it, even if the problem persists. Finally, ask for advice from someone you trust regarding what you can do about all "C" worries. If nothing, move the worry to the "A" category. If you identify something practical you can do about the worry, move it to the "B" category; and then respond accordingly.

2. Use the concept of being yoked to Christ (Matthew 11:28-30) as good reason to turn worry and concern about things you can't control over to the Lord. Since the one you are yoked to does everything perfectly, and has all power, you can rest assured that whatever He is involved in will ultimately work to your advantage, as well as to the advantage of others you care about. You therefore have no need to worry about anything that is beyond your control.

3. Personalize and then memorize D & C 100:1. Review the scripture every time you are tempted to worry about your family or something that is happening at home.

4. Disconnect worry from caring. Our Eternal Parents care about us deeply; but it's doubtful that they fret and stew about us like we sometimes do when people we love have problems. Otherwise, eternal life would be pretty horrible. Apparently, we all need to learn sooner or later how to love without worrying.

5. If you are prayerful and committed but can't think of anything constructive and practical that you can do to solve a problem, then decide that there is no need to worry about it. If the issue is something that you should worry about, as long as you are committed and prayerful, the Lord will make that fact clear to you. What you need to do about the worry will be made obvious.

As you work through the kinds of problems identified above, remember several important factors which can impact how successful you are.

1. Pick just one or two things to work on at a time. Don't overwhelm yourself by trying to fix everything at once.

2. Be persistent. If you try a suggestion for a short time and it doesn't seem to help; keep at it diligently for at least a three week period. Habits of thinking and behaving typically take a long time to change.
3. Call on the spiritual help that is available. But don't just pray for relief from a problem. Pray for guidance regarding how to solve the problem and help in following your plan.

CONCLUDING COMMENT

Those who are serving and those who have served know firsthand that full-time missions are difficult; but then, so is life in general. Since it's designed to be a test and learning opportunity, it's bound to be extra difficult at times. Quoting President Hinckley, "Anyone who imagines that bliss is normal is going to waste a lot of time running around shouting that he's been robbed" (Gordon B. Hinckley, "God Shall Give You Knowledge by His Holy Spirit", BYU Devotional, September, 1973.). Whether on a mission or at some other point in life, we will all have our share of struggles; but we are not left alone. The Lord said, "Be patient in afflictions, for thou shalt have many; but endure them, for lo, I am with thee, even unto the end of thy days" (D&C 24:8). Nothing could be more comforting than to know that, as we seek Him, the Lord will be with us every step of the way.

My hope and prayer is that the ideas in this book reflect truths taught in scripture, both canonized scripture and the inspired words of apostles and prophets. I hope that by following the counsel from these sources, missionaries, and all of us, will avoid the common mistakes that can ruin a mission, or one's life. I further hope that readers will recognize that even if they are currently enmeshed in one or more of the mistakes identified, it is not too late to change. Thanks to the atonement, we have a continuing opportunity to get it right; and great blessings are still available. We can still be perfected in Christ; at which point all emotional and mental health problems will be a thing of the past.

We will then have discovered the ultimate remedy for relief from all emotional and mental ills.

Of that day and regarding the process to get there, the prophet Moroni taught:

> "Yea, come unto Christ, and be perfected in him, and deny yourselves of all ungodliness; and if ye shall deny yourselves of all ungodliness, and love God with all your might, mind and strength, then is his grace sufficient for you, that by his grace ye may be perfect in Christ; and if by the grace of God ye are perfect in Christ, ye can in nowise deny the power of God, And again, if ye by the grace of God are perfect in Christ, and deny not his power, then are ye sanctified in Christ by the grace of God, through the shedding of the blood of Christ, which is in the covenant of the Father unto the remission of your sins, that ye become holy, without spot" (Moroni 10:32-22).